RED SOX

in 5s and 10s

BOSTON'S AGONY AND ECSTASY

BILL NOWLIN

Foreword by Rico Petrocelli

THE
History
PRESS

Published by The History Press
Charleston, SC
www.historypress.com

Front cover, top left: Leslie Jones photograph, Boston Public Library; *top right*: Bill Nowlin photo; *bottom left*: Bill Nowlin photo; *bottom right*: Leslie Jones photograph, Boston Public Library.
Back cover, top: Bill Nowlin photo; *bottom*: Bill Nowlin photo.

First published 2020

Manufactured in the United States

ISBN 9781467145084

Library of Congress Control Number: 2019956048

CONTENTS

FOREWORD

I was very fortunate to play for the Red Sox my whole career and to spend over fifty years in the Boston area. I think I've read just about every book published about the Red Sox—books about Red Sox players and books about the great Red Sox teams that have won four World Series championships. You probably have read many of them yourself. However, the newest book, *Red Sox in 5s and 10s*, by Bill Nowlin, is, in my opinion, one of the best.

Bill is no slouch when it comes to Red Sox history. He's written six books on Ted Williams, biographies of Johnny Pesky and Tom Yawkey and a great book on the 2004 World Champs. He's edited books on the '67, '75, and '86 teams for SABR. He knows the Red Sox.

This book is a must-read for all Red Sox fans. Bill gives us nine categories that he feels are the best and worst accomplishments of former Red Sox players. You'll get not only statistics but also tidbits about the players themselves. I especially like Bill's "Top 5 Home Openers" and "Top 10 Debuts by a Red Sox Player." Bill puts Daniel Nava's first-pitch grand-slam home run in 2010 and Billy Rohr's near no-hitter in 1967 as two of his favorites.

He does the same with hitters, pitchers, fielding, the best rookie seasons and much more. Bill's final category is called "Best of the Best." He gives us the Red Sox players and teams he feels are the best of all time. You may disagree with him on some of his picks, but it will bring back memories of some of the greatest players and teams in Red Sox history. Bill has done a terrific job writing *Red Sox in 5s and 10s*. I know you'll enjoy this book as much as I have.

—Rico Petrocelli

ACKNOWLEDGEMENTS

This book was inspired by Brian Wright's book *Mets in 10s*, published by The History Press in 2018. I worked with Brian on a book for SABR, *Met-rospectives*, as he was wrapping up *Mets in 10s*. Thanks to Jim Prime for getting me started writing for books when we put together *Ted Williams: A Tribute* more than twenty years ago. And thanks to Mike Kinsella of The History Press for welcoming this book.

I

OPENING DAYS

OPENING THE SEASON IN STYLE

Top 5 Home Openers

Opening Day in Boston has always been an event. It's the true start of spring in many a mind—though the temperature on, say, Opening Day 2018 (April 5) was forty degrees. It cooled down by the later innings; the game lasted twelve innings, ending at 6:00 p.m. on the nose, but the Red Sox won it in a walk off (the first of seven walk-off wins in 2018), beating Tampa Bay, 3–2. And we know how the 2018 season turned out.

In 1967, Opening Day was postponed with the temperature at thirty-five degrees and winds gusting to forty miles per hour. When they played the next day, April 12, the Red Sox won, 5–4. Any Opening Day win for the Red Sox is a good win.

Tuesday, April 9, 2019, was probably on many folks' calendars as a bright day. The 2018 Red Sox had won 119 games, including the World Series, pretty much waltzing through the postseason. Opening Day was when the champions were to get their rings and see the World Championship flag raised on the center-field flagpole, and fans could just generally exult in the team having won four World Series in fifteen years. But they had entered the home opener after 11 games on the road and were 3-8. And then they lost this game, too. That they had scored the first run of the game, and then the second, didn't really matter all that much when the final score was posted: Blue Jays 7, Red Sox 5.

The Sox have a pretty good record in home openers: 72-51.

They also have a pretty good record in the twenty-eight home openers when they have hosted the Yankees: 15-13. But here's something unexpected:

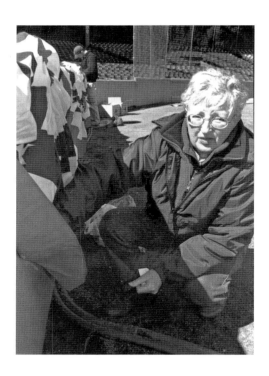

Mary Alden installing bunting at Fenway Park in preparation for Opening Day. *Bill Nowlin photo.*

their record was 8-13 through 1960, but after the league expanded in 1961, they have won every one of the seven times they've hosted the Yankees for the Fenway home opener: 1970, 1971, 1973, 1985, 2005, 2010 and 2011. Bring 'em back!

Here are our top picks for the best home openers in Red Sox history.

1. April 10, 1998 (Red Sox 9, Mariners 7)

The Red Sox opened the year on the West Coast—in Oakland, Seattle, and Anaheim—and returned home with a 3-5 record. The home opener started at 3:12 on a Friday afternoon. It was both Good Friday and the first day of Passover, and the Red Sox elected not to serve beer at the ballpark. The Sox had lost two out of three to the Mariners and were now facing starter Randy Johnson. Neither team scored for the first three, but center fielder Damon Buford hit a two-run homer off Johnson in the bottom of the fourth. In the top of the sixth, however, Seattle unsettled Sox starter Brian Rose and put three runs across. They built on their lead, adding two more runs in the eighth and then two more in the top of the ninth. With the score 7–2, the park was emptying out. Heathcliff Slocumb relieved Randy Johnson. A single, a walk and a double gave the Red Sox a run. Another former Red Sox pitcher, Tony

Fossas, faced one batter and walked him. The bases were loaded, and there was still nobody out. Seattle skipper Lou Piniella brought in future Red Sox reliever Mike Timlin. Nomar Garciaparra singled to center, making it 7–4. Bases still loaded. Then Timlin hit John Valentin, 7–5. A well-placed single might be all it took to tie things up. Piniella beckoned in lefty Paul Spoljaric to pitch to Mo Vaughn (who had struck out three times in the game and been hit by a pitch.) Second pitch: grand slam. Peter Gammons wrote in the *Boston Globe* that there were "about 13,000 remaining" of the 32,805 attendees. Those who stuck around to the end saw a finale they'll never forget.

And they heard something, too. Kevin Friend of BCN Productions had a new gig at Fenway; he'd worked in a similar capacity at the Boston Garden for a few years. Now he was in charge of the music played in the park. The moment after Mo launched the ball into the right-field grandstand seats, Friend put on "Dirty Water" by the Standells. "Aw-oh, Boston, you're my home!" It became the Red Sox victory anthem. A new tradition was born.[1]

2. April 6, 1973 (Red Sox 15, Yankees 5)

For most Red Sox fans, seeing the Sox give the Yankees a shellacking and win by ten runs has to rank right up there as a very satisfying way to kick off a season. This was, as it happened, the first major-league game to use a designated hitter (DH). In this case, the players designated to hit were New York's Ron Blomberg and Boston's Orlando Cepeda. Between them, they were 1-for-9. Cepeda was 0-for-6. Luis Tiant pitched for the Red Sox and faced Blomberg in the top of the first inning, with the bases loaded. Blomberg didn't hit; he walked, driving in a run. The Yankees took a 3–0 lead when Felipe Alou doubled behind him. Yastrzemski hit a solo homer in the bottom of the first, and Carlton Fisk hit a two-run homer in the bottom of the second. The Sox scored another pair of runs in the second. When Fisk (who had been AL Rookie of the Year in 1972) came up in the fourth inning, he hit a grand slam. For some unfathomable reason, Fisk (who already had a double, two home runs, and six RBIs) was hit by a pitch when he came up to bat in the sixth. Fifteen runs on twenty hits. The Sox won the next three games from the Yankees, too.

Red Sox Hall of Famer Luis Tiant at the 2018 Old-Timers' Game. *Bill Nowlin photo.*

3. April 14, 1978 (Red Sox 5, Rangers 4 [ten innings])
The Sox started 1978 2-3 on the road. The Texas Rangers met them in Boston and scored once in the second and once in the third. The Red Sox evened it up with one in the fourth and one in the sixth. The one-run pattern continued, with Texas scoring once in the seventh and once in the eighth. In the bottom of the eighth, Butch Hobson homered. Jerry Remy singled, advanced to second and third on a passed ball and a groundout, then scored on Jim Rice's single. Game tied. Sox starter Dennis Eckersley pitched into the tenth, but two singles put runners on first and second with two outs. Dick Drago was brought in to relieve—and threw a wild pitch. Both baserunners advanced. But Drago struck out Toby Harrah. Hobson singled to lead off the bottom of the tenth. Remy bunted him to second, and he scored two batters later on a walk-off single by Jim Rice.

4. April 10, 2007 (Red Sox 14, Mariners 3)
This game makes our list simply because it was the biggest blowout win among home openers—the Sox scored eleven more runs than the visiting team. In terms of run differential, that's one more than the 1973 game against the Yankees. There was never any suspense. The Red Sox scored four runs in the first, three in the second, one in the third, three in the fourth, and two more in the fifth.

In the midst of all this crossing of the plate, the Mariners scored only once, and Boston starter Josh Beckett allowed only two hits in the first seven innings. The only home run was hit by J.D. Drew. The Red Sox hammered out seven doubles, though. Even with all the runs they scored, they left eight on base.

5. April 20, 1912 (Red Sox 7, New York Highlanders 6 [eleven innings])
The very first game ever played at Fenway Park was a win, which is good. It was also a nice game from a rivalry standpoint. The Sox beat the Highlanders (soon to become the Yankees), 7–6, in eleven innings. New York led 5–1 after three innings, but Boston scored three runs in the bottom of the fourth, so skipper Jake Stahl asked Charley Hall to pitch in relief of starter Buck O'Brien. Hall worked the rest of the game—seven innings of long relief. He also drew a base on balls and scored the tying run in the sixth. With darkness approaching (the park didn't have lights for more than thirty years), the eleventh was certain to be the final inning. It might have gone into the books as a tie. But Sox second baseman Steve Yerkes reached first and then second on two errors by third baseman Cozy Dolan. He took third on a passed ball, and Tris Speaker scorched a single between shortstop and third to win the game.

FIVE OTHER SPECIAL HOME OPENERS

1. April 12, 1916 (Red Sox 2, Philadelphia Athletics 1)

The Red Sox were the reigning world champions, and this was the first game of another pennant-winning season and World Series win. Starting for Boston was Babe Ruth, 18-8 in 1915 and on his way to a 23-12 season in 1916, with a league-leading 1.75 earned run average. The one run he gave up in this game was unearned, in the top of the ninth. After five scoreless innings, the Red Sox had scored single runs in the sixth and seventh. Rube Foster relieved Ruth in the ninth and secured the final two outs of the game.

2. April 21, 1921 (Red Sox 1, Washington Senators 0)

Neither team wasted time playing this game. The whole game took only one hour and seventeen minutes to play. Part of the reason was that Red Sox starter Sam Jones allowed only two base hits and walked just two men. There were no errors. The lone run of the game was scored in the second inning. Stuffy McInnis doubled but was tagged out trying to reach third on Everett Scott's grounder. A weak roller to third base died on the field but in fair territory. Then Jones himself slapped another one on the same route, but this one hit third base—hard—and bounced away from the third baseman while Scott scored.

3. April 20, 1946 (Boston 2, Philadelphia Athletics 1)

The 1946 Red Sox wouldn't be denied; after the first two dozen games, they were 21-3. Tex Hughson allowed just one third-inning run on eight hits. Philadelphia's Dick Fowler was stingier; he allowed just two hits in the whole game. The first was in the first. With one out, Johnny Pesky and Ted Williams walked, and Pesky scored all the way from second base when Bobby Doerr hit into what looked like a standard 6-4-3 double play. But the

Bobby Doerr (*left*) and Johnny Pesky at unveiling of *The Teammates* statue outside Fenway Park being interviewed by Dick Flavin. *Bill Nowlin photo.*

Athletics were a hair too slow to execute, and Doerr was safe at first base. A throw home failed to catch Pesky. In the bottom of the eighth inning, Pesky homered just ten feet to the left of the right-field foul pole (the pole now known as the "Pesky pole.") The 2–1 score held.

4. April 18, 1952 (Red Sox 5, Philadelphia Athletics 4 [ten innings])
Walk-off wins in extra innings always serve as a nice way to start a season. With two runs in the top of the second and one in the fifth, the Athletics were looking good. The Sox scored just once in the sixth and saw Philadelphia match that in the eighth, giving them a 4–1 lead heading into the bottom of the ninth. Pesky walked. Pinch-hitter Clyde Vollmer singled him to second. Dom DiMaggio—who had failed to get the ball out of the infield in four tries—squirted one past the shortstop. Pesky scored. Jimmy Piersall doubled off the Wall to make it 4–3, and DiMaggio then scored the tying run on a fielder's choice. It was tied in the tenth when Faye Throneberry walked, reached second on Billy Goodman's single, and scored when Vollmer singled to left field.

5. April 26, 1995 (Red Sox 9, Minnesota Twins 0)
This game was special because all of major-league baseball had been on strike since the first part of August 1994. Just to be able to see baseball again at Fenway for the first time since August 7 was a treat. It had been 261 days, more than two-thirds of a year. Given that players were rusty without their usual spring training, each manager used five pitchers in the game. Aaron Sele started for the Red Sox and worked the first five, allowing just one hit. Four relievers were paraded out, each one working just one inning. The Twins got only one other hit in the game, while the Red Sox piled up nine runs—one in the second, one in the fifth, and then seven runs in the bottom of the sixth. Mo Vaughn drove in three. Mike Greenwell was 4-for-5 and drove in two. José Canseco drove in two. From May 13 on, the Red Sox held first place all season long but were swept by the Indians in the AL Division Series.

A ROAD OPENER

April 8, 1969 (Red Sox 5, Orioles 4 [twelve innings], at Memorial Stadium, Baltimore)
There is one road opener we would like to note, for a couple of reasons. First of all, this game represented the return of Tony Conigliaro after his horrific beaning in August 1967. The score was 2–2 after nine. "Tony C" hit

a two-run homer to give the Red Sox a 4–2 lead in the top of the tenth, but then Frank Robinson hit a two-run homer to re-tie the game. In the twelfth, Conig walked, went to second on a single, to third base on another walk, and scored on a sacrifice fly. The Orioles were set down 1-2-3.

As a postscript, we note that the Red Sox took thirteen innings to play the season's second game (Baltimore won, 2–1) and then needed fifteen innings to complete their third game, in Cleveland, beating the Indians, 2–1.

2

A FEW OPENING DAYS TO FORGET

The Worst Home Openers

1. April 16, 1968 (Detroit Tigers 9, Red Sox 2)
We won't devote nearly as many words to losses as to victories. This is, after all, a book for Red Sox fans to enjoy. Once upon a time, in the last century, most Red Sox fans knew little but anguish. This was far from their worst loss, but as home openers go, the seven-run differential represents the most lopsided defeat in a home opener. The Sox scored first, but only once, in the second inning. They added one more run in the seventh. What did them in was the eight-run fourth inning, all eight runs charged to starter Ray Culp.

2. April 18, 1950 (Yankees 15, Red Sox 10)
This one looked like a laugher. The Red Sox scored three runs in the first, one in the second and then five more in the fourth inning. It was Boston 9, New York 0, until the top of the sixth, when the Yankees scored four. Even that didn't seem too bad. After all, the Red Sox still held a five-run lead, and Boston added another run in the seventh, 10–4. Mel Parnell was pitching for the Red Sox. Everything went wrong in the top of the eighth. By the time the inning was over, Parnell had been charged with four more runs, and the Red Sox had trotted out four relievers to try to stop the onslaught. The Yankees scored nine. They tacked on two more in the top of the ninth. The twenty-five runs scored are the most ever in a Red Sox home opener.

3. April 11, 1928 (Washington Senators 8, Red Sox 4)

The worst thing about this game wasn't the score per se. Down 7–0 after the first five innings, the Sox at least scored a few runs to make it respectable. It was just another Red Sox loss, one of ninety-six losses in 1928. What was most dispiriting about it is that it was the fifth home opener in a row they had lost (1924, 1925, 1926, 1927, and 1928). The 1920s was the most dismal of decades for the Red Sox. In 1925, they finished last and did so again in 1926 and 1927, and then in 1928, 1929, and 1930. The team actually had won the day before, when Washington hosted them for the first game of the year, but that was the last time all year the Sox were any higher than fourth place. Most of the time, they were in the cellar.

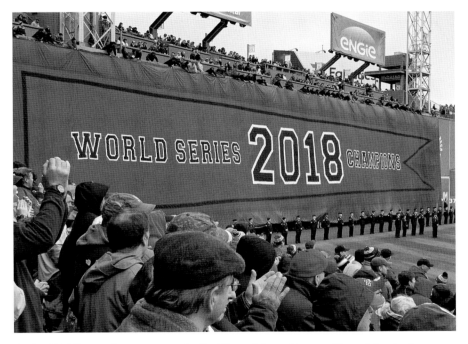

At the 2019 Fenway home opener, the Red Sox celebrated by unveiling a Monster-long banner celebrating the 2018 World Championship. *Bill Nowlin photo.*

II

RED SOX PLAYER DEBUTS

TOP 10 DEBUTS BY A RED SOX PLAYER

1. Daniel Nava (June 12, 2010)
It's hard to imagine how one could ever top this debut. This afternoon, with the reigning National League champion Phillies at Fenway, Daniel Nava came to bat in the bottom of the second inning. The Phillies held a 2–1 lead. Red Sox broadcaster Joe Castiglione had talked with Nava before the game and told him he'd only ever see one first pitch in the big leagues. Joe Blanton (12-8 for the Phils in 2009) had allowed a home run and then three consecutive singles. The bases were loaded, and there was nobody out. Nava swung at the first pitch he saw and homered—a grand slam—into the Red Sox bullpen.[2]

2. Billy Rohr (April 14, 1967)
Left-hander Billy Rohr threw his first pitch in the big leagues at Yankee Stadium. Horace Clark grounded out. Rohr didn't allow a hit in the first inning, or the second, or the third. In the bottom of the fourth, he walked two but still hadn't allowed a base hit. In fact, after eight full innings, Rohr was one inning away from a no-hitter, and the Red Sox were winning against Whitey Ford, 3–0. In the bottom of the ninth, Tom Tresh lined out to left field, and a spectacular diving catch by Carl Yastrzemski kept Rohr's no-hitter alive. Joe Pepitone flied out to right. Rohr was one out away from a no-hitter, but Yankee catcher Elston Howard hit a clean single to right-center. Rohr retired the next man up and had to settle for a one-hit shutout.

3. Dave "Boo" Ferriss (April 29, 1945)

Facing the first three batters for the Philadelphia A's, Ferriss walked the bases loaded. He got out of the inning without giving up a run and actually won the game, a five-hit, 2–0 shutout. He was 3-for-3 at the plate and scored the second of the two Red Sox runs. His second start was against the Yankees, at Fenway on May 6. He shut them out, too, allowing seven hits. And he got halfway into his third game—against the Tigers—before he gave up his first run, ending a string of twenty-two-plus consecutive scoreless innings.

4. Larry Pape (July 6, 1909)

The twenty-three-year-old right-hander's major-league pitching debut saw him work at Fenway Park and throw a four-hit, 2–0 shutout against the visiting Washington Nationals. Seven Red Sox pitchers have thrown shutouts their first time out, but Pape remains the only one to do so in a home game.[3] Pape played his full major-league career with the Red Sox and never had a losing record; in parts of three seasons, he was 13-9.

5. George Edward "Lefty" Hockette (September 17, 1934)

Hockette matched Pape, with a two-hit shutout in St. Louis (he had a no-hitter through seven innings). He was only in the majors for parts of two years and was 4-4 in twenty-three games (seven starts). In November 1935, he was part of a transaction that led to future Hall of Famer Bobby Doerr coming to the Red Sox.

6. Eddie Pellagrini (April 22, 1946)

Boston native Eddie Pellagrini made his major-league debut, filling in during the fifth inning after Johnny Pesky was beaned by a fastball. Pelly's first big-league at-bat came in the seventh inning in a game tied 4–4. Sid Hudson was pitching for Washington. Pellagrini hit a game-winning home run over the left-field wall. The Sox beat the Senators, 5–4.

7. Frank Malzone (September 20, 1955)

His first ten at-bats all came in a doubleheader against the Orioles. The Red Sox lost both games, but Malzone was 6-for-10 on the day. Over the course of his career—all with the Red Sox—the third baseman was named to eight All-Star squads.

8. Tony Conigliaro (April 17, 1964)

Another local kid made good, this time it was the home debut for nineteen-year-old Tony Conigliaro. He turned on the first pitch he was thrown and hit it over everything in left field—out of the park. He hit 23 more homers that year, setting a record for the most home runs ever hit by a teenager. From his SABR bio: "When he led the league in homers with 32 the following year, he became the youngest player ever to take the home-run crown. When he hit home run number 100, during the first game of a doubleheader on July 23, 1967, he was only twenty-two—the youngest AL player to reach the 100-homer plateau."[4]

9. Ted Cox (September 18, 1977)

Boston played in Baltimore and won, 10–4. Three of the runs scored were thanks to twenty-two-year-old Cox of the Sox, who was 4-for-4. The next day, the Red Sox hosted the Yankees, and Cox singled his first two times at bat—six base hits in his first six big-league at-bats.

10. Eduardo Rodriguez (May 28, 2015)

In his debut, Rodriguez threw seven and two-thirds innings of three-hit baseball without allowing a run to the Texas Rangers. In his second game, on June 3, he allowed just one run on two hits in seven innings of work. Very good, of course, but it may not seem that remarkable. However, no pitcher since at least 1900 had ever worked at least two innings in his first two appearances and given up three or fewer hits, allowing no more than one run. And he made it even more difficult for any would-be challenger by throwing six innings in his third appearance—no runs and just three hits.

4

PLAYERS WHO PERFORMED PARTICULARLY WELL IN THEIR RED SOX DEBUTS

There are a number of players who started their careers elsewhere but made a very good first impression when debuting for the Red Sox.

1. Jake Jones (June 15, 1947)
Jones had played three-plus seasons with the White Sox but came to the Red Sox on June 14 in a trade for Rudy York. The next day, the Red Sox hosted the White Sox for a doubleheader at Fenway Park. Boston held a 6–3 lead over Chicago, but Jones contributed a seventh-inning solo home run to provide an additional insurance run. In the second game, it was 4–4 after six innings and remained so until the bottom of the ninth. With two outs and the bases loaded, Jones hit a grand slam. Welcome to Boston.

2. Matt Young (April 12, 1992)
In Cleveland, Young walked the first man he faced, Kenny Lofton, who came around to score on a stolen base and an error. In the third inning, another run scored on a pair of walks and two outs. Young was losing the game, 2–0, and he still hadn't given up a base hit. He never did. He pitched eight full innings, a complete game, since the Indians held a 2–1 lead and there was no need for them to bat in the ninth. His catcher, John Flaherty, had caught a no-hitter in his major-league debut. Except the Powers That Be declared the game—in which the Indians never managed a base hit—was not really a no-hitter, because Young hadn't gone nine.

3. Hideo Nomo (April 4, 2001)

They couldn't figure out a way to take this one away. Hideo Nomo had pitched for four other major-league teams before he came to the Red Sox. On the second day of the year, Nomo threw a no-hitter against the Orioles. He allowed three bases on balls, and there was a Sox error, but no one scored on him. It was 3–0, Boston.

4. Darnell McDonald (April 20, 2010)

He came into the bottom of the eighth inning as a pinch-hitter in a game the Sox were losing to the Rangers, 6–4. With Jason Varitek on base, McDonald homered to tie it. He came up again in the bottom of the ninth. There were two outs, but the bases were loaded. He hammered a ball off the left-field wall, winning the game.

III

ROOKIE SEASONS AND GRAND FINALES

5

BEST ROOKIE SEASONS

One healthy indicator of the best rookie seasons of Sox players would be the list of six Boston players who have won the American League Rookie of the Year Award. Right?

Here they are:

1. Walt Dropo (1950)
In his rookie year, despite not being called up from the minor leagues until early May, first baseman Walt Dropo led both leagues, driving in 144 runs. That total was just one short of the major-league rookie record, set by Dropo's teammate Ted Williams in 1939. Dropo led the American League in total bases with 326. He hit 34 home runs, 3 behind league-leader Al Rosen and 2 ahead of Joe DiMaggio. Dropo got fifteen votes for Rookie of the Year, to six for pitcher Whitey Ford of the Yankees and two for Chico Carrasquel of the White Sox. Remarkably, another Red Sox player—Vern Stephens—tied Dropo with those 144 RBIs in 1950. This was the year the Red Sox scored 1,027 runs. Williams might well have topped them all (he had 83 RBIs at the All-Star Break), but he broke his elbow in the All-Star Game and played fewer than 60 percent of the season's games. Dropo struggled in 1951 and spent a good part of the season in the minors; he drove in only 57 runs for Boston.

2. Don Schwall (1961)
The tall (six-foot, six-inch) right-hander was 15-7 in 1961 with a 3.22 earned run average. It was a close vote for ROY that saw Schwall (seven votes) edge

out Kansas City's shortstop Dick Howser (six votes). Three other players each received two votes: Frank Robinson, Schwall teammate Chuck Schilling, and Lee Thomas. Jake Wood received one vote. As seems to occur more often than one might expect, the sophomore season saw him slip: Schwall was 9-15 (4.94) and he was traded to the Pirates in November, part of the deal that brought Dick Stuart to Boston. Only once again did Schwall win as many as nine games in a season.

3. Carlton Fisk (1972)

Catcher Carlton Fisk was voted into the National Baseball Hall of Fame in 2000. Voting wasn't even close in his rookie year; Fisk won every one of the twenty-four first-place votes for Rookie of the Year, a unanimous choice. He hit .293 with 22 homers and 61 RBIs. He scored 74 runs and helped propel the Red Sox through a strike-shortened season that saw Boston fall just a half game short of the Detroit Tigers in the AL East standings. There was no wild card at the time. Fisk won a Gold Glove for his defense and enjoyed the first of his eleven career All-Star designations.

4. Fred Lynn (1975)

Fred Lynn pulled off the rare feat of being named both Rookie of the Year and Most Valuable Player in the same year. In the MVP voting, he received twenty-two of the twenty-four first-place votes. The ROY voting was not that lopsided, but he still got more than twice as many points as the second-place finisher. Teammate Jim Rice ranked a close third. He hit .331 and had a league-leading OPS (On-Base Percentage plus Slugging) of .967. He led both leagues in doubles (47) and the AL in runs scored (103). For nine years in a row, Lynn was an American League All-Star, though the latter three of those years were with the Angels, to whom he was traded after the 1980 campaign. The Sox centerfielder was part of one of the greatest Red Sox outfields of all time, flanked by Rice in left field and Dwight Evans in right.

5. Nomar Garciaparra (1997)

Shortstop Nomar Garciaparra's first four seasons with the Red Sox saw him hit for a higher batting average each year than the one before. Starting with his rookie season's .306, he went to .323, then .357, and then .372. In the latter two years, he won back-to-back batting championships. Two more years, averaging an increase of 22 points a year, would have projected him to hit .394 and then .416. That didn't happen. Injury limited him to only twenty-one games (and a .289 batting average) in 2001, and while he never again failed to hit over .300 for the Red Sox, he was also never quite the same. It was quite the comedown when GM Theo Epstein boldly traded one of the most popular players in Red Sox history in late 2004—and the trade seemed to help the Red Sox win their first World Series in eighty-six years. Nomar drove in 98 runs in his rookie year; four times he surpassed 100 in the years to come. In 1997, he received every first-place vote in the ROY balloting.

6. Dustin Pedroia (2007)

Red Sox fans love an energetic, hustling rookie—and Dustin Pedroia soon picked up the mantle that Nomar had worn. Pedroia, playing second base, won twenty-four of the twenty-eight first-place votes for ROY, and his overall point total of 132 overshadowed the second-place 56 for Delmon Young. Pedroia hit .317 and scored 86 runs. He followed it up by winning the MVP voting the next year, in 2008. He helped the Sox reach the postseason in 2007, a year in which they never once sank to as low as second place in their division. Batting leadoff in Game One of the World Series, he homered over Fenway Park's left-field wall. History is still being written as this book goes to print, but he was a key component of the 2013 campaign that netted the Red Sox another World Championship. He won a third ring in 2018, though injuries kept him out almost all year.

Dustin Pedroia on the field with some young fans during a family friendly Fenway event. *Bill Nowlin photo.*

7. Dave "Boo" Ferriss (1945)

We should mention him once more. He won his first eight decisions, beating every one of the other seven American League clubs in the process. At the end of his rookie year, he was 21-10 with 26 complete games, including 5 shutouts and an earned run average of 2.96.

THERE ARE PLENTY OF others who came close to being named Rookie of the Year—most recently, Andrew Benintendi, who placed second in the voting in 2017. But the Yankees' Aaron Judge hit 52 homers. Tough to compete with that—though Benintendi no doubt takes some solace in earning a World Championship ring in his sophomore year, something that has so far eluded Mr. Judge. Here are a few others who were denied this honor.

Ted Williams (1939)

Why didn't Ted Williams win the Rookie of the Year Award in 1939? He certainly had one of the best seasons any rookie ever had. He set two rookie records that year, both of which still stand eighty years later. As noted earlier, he drove in 145 runs. He also drew 107 bases on balls. Williams refused to swing at bad pitches and probably cost himself a few home runs or RBIs, but his patience paid off, and he finished his career with another record he still holds: the highest career on-base percentage of anyone who ever played the game (.482). That means that almost half the time he came to the plate, he got on base. In 1939, his 344 total bases also placed him first. He homered 31 times. Why didn't he win the Rookie of the Year Award? It didn't exist. The award was initiated in 1947.

Ted Williams in his rookie year, 1939. He played right field and set a still-standing major-league record with 145 RBIs. *Leslie Jones photograph, Boston Public Library.*

Johnny Pesky is another Red Sox rookie who fell short for the same reason. He led all of baseball with 205 base hits in his 1942 rookie year. He hit 208 in 1946 (after three years asway from baseball due to war) and 207 in 1947. For three years in a row, he had more than 200 base hits.

Cy Young did pretty good in his first year with the franchise. In 1901, he was 33-10 with an ERA of 1.62. He already had eleven major-league seasons under his belt. He may have been a rookie with the Red Sox, but by no means was he a rookie in the usual sense of the word. He'd been pitching in the National League since 1890 and already had ten 20-win seasons under his belt. As we will see later, his WAR (Wins above Replacement) of 12.6 was the highest WAR ever calculated for any Red Sox player.

THE GRANDEST FINALES

Best Player Final Seasons

1. David Ortiz (2016)

It would be pretty difficult to go out with a better final season than David Ortiz had in 2016. He'd announced it would be his final year before the season began. All he did in 2016 was lead the league in runs batted in (127) and all of baseball in slugging percentage (.620) and OPS (On-Base Percentage plus Slugging (1.021). He led both leagues in doubles (48). His 38 homers placed him in the top ten. He won his seventh Silver Slugger and was named to his tenth All-Star squad.

2. Ted Williams (1960)

Had Ted retired after the 1957 season, or even 1958, this might have been a no-brainer. He won the batting title both years, hitting an extremely impressive .388 in 1957—at age thirty-nine. He kept playing, however, and suffered a cramped nerve in his neck in spring training in 1959. He never recovered that year, batting a pedestrian .254. After demanding a 30 percent pay cut for himself for 1960 (these were the days before a powerful player's association), Williams boosted his average back over .300, to .316, and most notably hit a home run in his final at-bat.

3. Pedro Martínez (2004)

Not bad. In fact, very good. The year 2004 was not his best, but he was 16-9, placing fourth in the Cy Young Award voting. And the very last game he pitched for the Red Sox was Game Three of the 2004 World Series. He threw seven innings, allowing just three base hits and not even one run. The Red Sox won the game, 4–1, and the next day won their first World Championship since 1918.

4. Curt Schilling (2007)

There was 2004 for Curt Schilling, too: he was 21-6 and came in second in Cy Young voting, topping Pedro's performance that year. He was injured in Game One of the ALCS against the Yankees, and only a temporary medical procedure permitted him to come back (and win) the "Bloody Sock Game" (Game Six), then to win Game Two of the World Series. His final season in the books is 2007, when he helped the Sox get to the postseason once again and won one game in each round: Game Three of the ALDS, Game Six of the ALCS, and Game Two of the World Series, a 2–1 win over the Rockies. He was signed for 2008 but unable to play. "Big Schill" left the game with some of the best postseason stats of any pitcher in baseball history: 11-2 with a 2.23 ERA.

IV

RED SOX PITCHERS

BEST SINGLE-GAME PERFORMANCES

1. Cy Young (May 5, 1904)

It would be pretty hard to improve on a perfect game. One could imagine a game of eighty-one pitches, every one a strike, but that's not going to happen. The third perfect game in major-league history—and the first one in the so-called modern era—saw Cy Young set down twenty-seven Philadelphia Athletics in order, not a single one of them reaching first base. Boston won, 3–0. That same year, in August, Jesse Tannehill threw a no-hitter for Boston, but there's simply nothing that can match a perfect game.

Young's perfect game came in the midst of an incredible hitless innings streak. On April 25, he wrapped up a game without allowing a hit in the final three innings. On April 30, he worked seven innings in relief, not allowing a hit. Then he threw the perfect game on May 5. At that point, he had thrown 18 consecutive hitless innings. And he wasn't done. On May 11, he started and didn't allow a hit for 6⅓ innings. That adds up to 25⅓ consecutive hitless innings, a stretch in which he had secured outs from seventy-six batters before one finally got a base hit. Scoring on him was even harder; those innings fell within a stretch during which he threw 45⅔ consecutive scoreless innings. The May 11 game was a 1–0 fifteen-inning win.

Young threw another no-hitter for the Red Sox, on June 30, 1908. There's a reason he has an award named for him.

There have been sixteen or eighteen other no-hitters in Red Sox history, depending on one's definition of a no-hitter. That seems like a silly thing to write, but there are at least a couple of definitions. Major League Baseball has its definition, and then there is the commonsense definition. In 1991, three dozen no-hitters were wiped off the books because a new committee decided that a no-hitter had to last at least nine full innings. It's not quite that simple, but you can read about it here: https://www.nonohitters.com/near-no-hitters. Elsewhere in this book, you can read the story of Devern Hansack, who pitched a complete-game shutout for the Red Sox without giving up a hit, but his accomplishment was not recognized as a no-hitter because of something over which neither team had any control: it was truncated by rain after five innings.

2. Bill Dinneen (September 27, 1905)
An umpire threw a no-hitter for Boston? True. But he didn't become a full-time umpire until after his playing career was over, four years later, in 1909. Dinneen pitched and won 170 games from 1898 to 1909 but left his pitching career near the end of the 1909 season and ultimately umpired a very impressive 4,218 major-league ball games, through 1937. In 1902, 1903, and 1904, he was a 20-game winner each year for the Boston Americans, and he won three games in the 1903 World Series against Pittsburgh—the first World Series ever played. In 1905, he was only 12-14 with an ERA of 3.73 (it has been under 3.00 the three prior seasons). In his last two starts for Boston, he threw a no-hitter and then a 9–1 win. His no-hitter was a 2–0 win at the Huntington Avenue Grounds against the visiting White Sox. Dinneen had been out for the previous month with a sore arm but came back with a vengeance, striking out six. He walked the leadoff batter in the first and hit one in the second, but from that point on he didn't allow another man to reach base.

3. Ernie Shore (June 23, 1917)
In the twenty-first century, throwing a complete game has itself become rare. In his eight seasons with the Red Sox, Cy Young *averaged* more than thirty-four complete games a year. In his seven seasons with the Sox, Pedro Martínez threw a total of twenty-two complete games, just a little over three per year. In the last ten years before this book was written (2009 through 2018), the *entire Red Sox staff* threw forty-six complete games. And long relief is increasingly rare. Gone are the days of Dick Radatz, who in his four full seasons with the Red Sox averaged almost precisely two innings per relief appearance. All this is a lengthy preamble to the June 23, 1917 game that Babe Ruth started. In this game, a relief pitcher threw a perfect game for the Red Sox—or did he?

Ruth walked the first batter but was so angry at umpire Brick Owens's ball-four call that he got into it with the ump and actually struck him. Needless to say, Ruth was ejected. Shore was brought in to relieve. The baserunner tried to steal second base and was thrown out. Then Shore retired the next twenty-six batters he faced—every one of them—in order. Not a man reached base. With Shore on the mound, the Red Sox recorded twenty-seven consecutive outs. The Sox won, 4–0. For years, it was called a perfect game. But now it is no longer considered either a perfect game or a no-hitter. Could it have been any more perfect?

4. Roger Clemens (April 29, 1986)

There are no-hitters and there are no-hitters. With about three hundred of them in the history of major-league baseball, they are very special. But much rarer is the 20-strikeout game. There have even been twenty-three perfect games. But there have been only five 20-K games. Two of them were thrown by Roger Clemens of the Boston Red Sox, about ten years apart. The first was at Fenway on this date. Fortune saw him start against a team that was striking out at a record pace: the Seattle Mariners. He went to a 3-2 count on each one of the first three batters, then struck each one out—swinging. People noticed that. After 2 strikeouts in the top of the fourth, he had 8. Gorman Thomas fouled out to first base—but Don Baylor dropped the ball. And a significant number of Red Sox fans cheered, because it meant Roger could get another shot at adding a strikeout. He struck out Thomas. He struck out the side in the fifth (all three looking), then added 2 in the sixth and 2 more in the seventh. That was 16. When Spike Owen flied out to center to end the sixth, more than a few fans were yelling "Drop it!"[5] Clemens got 2 strikeouts in the eighth and hit 20 for a new major-league record with 2 more in the ninth. The last batter of the game grounded out, shortstop to first. Since Clemens set the record more than thirty years ago, it has been matched four times. Striking out 20 batters in a game is true dominance. The Red Sox made him work for the win, not scoring until the seventh. They won, 3–1.

5. Roger Clemens (September 18, 1996)

The next pitcher to record 20 Ks in a game was…Roger Clemens. In Detroit. Most Red Sox fans watched it on TV. Clemens struck out the side in the second and again in the fifth. By this time, he had an even dozen. If he could whiff eight of the next twelve batters—presuming the three runs the Red Sox had scored in the fourth held up and the Tigers needed to bat in the bottom of the ninth—he could hit 20. How likely was that? It had only ever been done once before, as noted. In the sixth, he recorded 3 more Ks. Now Sox fans were phoning friends, asking them if they were watching. It paid off. He got his 20 strikeouts, 15 of them swinging strikeouts. It was also the 100th complete game of his career. It took him 151 pitches, but he struck out 20 Tigers, tying his own record for most strikeouts in a nine-inning game. The win was number 192, tying him (with Cy Young) for the most wins in Red Sox history. The Sox won, 4–0, and the shutout was his thirty-eighth, also tying him with Young for the Red Sox record.

As it happens, Clemens started only two more games for the Red Sox. A free agent, he signed with the Toronto Blue Jays for 1997. He won Cy Youngs in 1997 and 1998, adding to the three he already had from his Red Sox days. He later won another pair while with the Yankees.

6. Pedro Martínez (September 11, 1999)

This game ranks high with many aficionados. No pitcher had ever struck out more Yankees in a game than Pedro Martínez did with the 17 Ks he registered against them this September evening at Yankee Stadium. He came into the game with a 20-4 record. The Yankees were six and a half games ahead of the Red Sox in the AL East. He hit the first batter he faced, Chuck Knoblauch, who was then cut down trying to steal second. In the bottom of the second, the Yankees took a 1–0 lead when Chili Davis homered. Pedro hit his stride by the fifth inning, striking out the side. The score hadn't changed, but then the Red Sox scored twice on a two-run homer by former Yankee Mike Stanley. When Pedro struck out the side again in the bottom of the seventh, he had whiffed an even dozen. He struck out two more in the eighth. The Yankees still hadn't collected a base hit off him other than the Davis home run. Boston added another run in the top of the ninth to give themselves a 3–1 lead. Pedro struck out the side in the bottom of the ninth, all three on swinging strikes. It was a one-hitter with 17 Ks.

7. Curt Schilling (October 19, 2004)

This was the famous "Bloody Sock Game." Curt Schilling was fortunate to be pitching this game at all. This was Game Six of the 2004 American League Championship Series against the New York Yankees. The Yankees had won Game One, 10–7, and knocked Schilling out after he gave up six runs in the first three innings. He had been pitching hurt. Back in Game One of the ALDS, fans saw him clutch his ankle when he bent down to try to catch a fifth-inning ball that rolled foul on the first-base line. It looked like he'd tweaked something. It was worse than that. He was pitching in real pain in ALCS Game One; it looked like he was done for the season. He'd ruptured his tendon sheath and dislocated the tendon in his right ankle. He was due for surgery. The Yankees won the first three games in the best-of-four ALCS, winning the third game, 19–8. Things could hardly have looked more dismal. The Yankees had won the 2003 ALCS, snatching what seemed likely victory away from the Red Sox. Now the Sox were without Schilling. But then the Red Sox rallied, winning both Game Four and Game Five, both in extra innings and both thanks to hits by David Ortiz. Ultimate victory was still unlikely; no team had ever come back to win a best-of-four series after losing the first three. And the Red Sox faced eighty-six years of history and purported curses. When it came right down to it, they just never seemed to be able to win it all.

Then team doctor Bill Morgan came up with an idea. He performed something of a surgical miracle, temporarily suturing the tendon in place.[6] Hoping it would hold, but also knowing that a misstep could do far worse damage and that an overcompensation could injure a shoulder or something else, Schilling took the mound in Game Six. This took real courage. During the game, television cameras quickly picked up that blood had seeped into Schilling's sock, visible to all. Schilling retired the first eight Yankees he faced. The Red Sox scored four times in the top of the fourth—a three-run homer by Mark Bellhorn *just* getting out, in fact, bouncing off a fan's chest and back onto the field. Schilling gave up one run, a solo homer in the bottom of the seventh, and then let the bullpen take over. Now the ALCS was tied. We all know who won Game Seven—and then swept St. Louis in the World Series. Not to be denied, Schilling worked six innings in Game Two of the World Series, giving up one unearned run. In 2007, he won one game in each playoff round in another Red Sox World Championship season.

8. Chris Sale (May 14, 2019)

Right-hander Chris Sale struck out the first six Rockies he faced this night at Fenway Park. Right out of the gate, he'd caught the attention of the home crowd—and, of course, the "K Men" in center field were keeping the tally for all to see. As had happened in Clemens's April 1986 game, when an out was recorded due to a fourth-inning grounder, there were audible boos from the crowd; everyone wanted another K. Sale also struck out the last two batters in the fifth and struck out the side in both the sixth and the seventh. After seven full innings, he had 17 strikeouts. Elementary math showed that with six outs to go, he might well get to 20 and go beyond. And he had not

Before a 2019 Chris Sale start, the K-Men carry on the tradition they began back in Pedro Martinez's day. *Bill Nowlin photo.*

walked even one batter. But the electronic scoreboard showed he'd thrown 108 pitches, and manager Alex Cora wanted to preserve Sale and not see him damage himself. He brought in another pitcher to take over. That might not have been a good move; there was a blown save, and the game went to extra innings, the Red Sox losing (despite an overall total of 24 strikeouts by the Boston staff). In his previous start, on May 8, Sale had struck out 14 (with no walks). He became the first Red Sox pitcher to post back-to-back starts with at least 10 Ks and 0 BB since Cy Young in September 1905. (He struck out ten Astros on his next start but walked five, matching a career worst.)

In addition to the ones noted above, the other no-hitters hurled by Red Sox pitchers are listed here.

August 17, 1904. Jesse Tannehill. Boston Americans 6, Chicago White Sox 0
June 30, 1908. Cy Young. Boston Red Sox 8, New York Highlanders 0
July 29, 1911. Smoky Joe Wood. Boston Red Sox 5, St. Louis Browns 0
June 21, 1916. Rube Foster. Boston Red Sox 2, New York Yankees 0; first no-hitter at Fenway

August 30, 1916. Dutch Leonard. Boston Red Sox 4, St. Louis Browns 0
June 3, 1918. Dutch Leonard. Boston Red Sox 5, Detroit Tigers 0
September 7, 1923. Howard Ehmke. Boston Red Sox 4, Philadelphia Athletics 0
July 14, 1956. Mel Parnell. Boston Red Sox 4, Chicago White Sox 0
June 26, 1962. Earl Wilson. Boston Red Sox 2, Los Angeles Angels 0
August 1, 1962. Bill Monbouquette. Boston Red Sox 1, Chicago White Sox
September 16, 1965. Dave Morehead. Boston Red Sox 2, Cleveland Indians 0
April 4, 2001. Hideo Nomo. Boston Red Sox 3, Baltimore Orioles 0
April 27, 2002. Derek Lowe. Boston Red Sox 10, Tampa Bay Devil Rays 0
September 1, 2007. Clay Buchholz. Boston Red Sox 10, Baltimore Orioles 0
May 19, 2008. Jon Lester. Boston Red Sox 7, Kansas City Royals 0

There have been two no-hitters thrown by Red Sox pitchers that are no longer recognized as such, following the 1991 committee decision. We have noted Devern Hansack's on October 1, 2006, which ended after five innings due to rain. The other was thrown by Matt Young at Cleveland Stadium on April 12, 1992. It was the first game of a doubleheader. Young pitched a complete game and allowed zero base hits. But he was not credited with a no-hitter. Why was that? The Red Sox lost the game, and since the Twins led, 2–1, after eight and one-third innings, there was no need for them to bat in the bottom of the ninth. They'd already won the

The media all want to talk with Derek Lowe after his no-hitter in 2002. *Bill Nowlin photo.*

game. Young walked leadoff batter Kenny Lofton, who then stole second, as he was wont to do. The Indians' Carlos Baerga hit a ball to Red Sox shortstop Luis Rivera, who committed an error and saw Lofton score. No hits, but the Indians had a 1–0 lead. Mark Lewis, the first Cleveland batter in the third, walked, and so did the second. A force play allowed Lewis to take third base. Baerga hit into a fielder's choice, and the Indians took a 2–0 lead. The Red Sox scored their only run of the game in the top of the fourth. Young pitched a game that's in the books as a complete game. He didn't allow a hit. But it's not considered a no-hitter because he didn't go the full nine innings. A pitcher could lose a game and get credited for a no-hitter, but—through no fault of his own—Young wasn't able to pitch the ninth on the road.

The committee ruling cuts both ways, of course. It also spared the Red Sox of being the victims in a perfect game thrown by Dean Chance at Metropolitan Stadium, Minneapolis, on August 6, 1967. The Sox lost the game, 2–0, so it still counted as a loss. But the game, like Hansack's, lasted only five innings due to rain.

Catching no-hitters? The record for catching no-hitters is four, shared by Jason Varitek of the Red Sox and Carlos Ruiz of the Philadelphia

Before a game, Jason Varitek's equipment bag is seen in the Red Sox dugout. "Tek" caught four (or five) no-hitters. *Bill Nowlin photo.*

Phillies. I submit that Tek caught five, if one includes the complete game thrown by Devern Hansack in which the pitcher allowed no hits. It's all a matter of definition. Varitek's "officially recognized" no-hitters caught are as follows:

Hideo Nomo. April 4, 2001. Red Sox 3, Baltimore 0, at Camden Yards
Derek Lowe. April 27, 2002. Red Sox 10, Tampa Bay 0, at Fenway Park
Clay Buchholz. September 1, 2007. Red Sox 10, Baltimore 0, at Fenway Park
Jon Lester. May 19, 2008. Red Sox 7, Kansas City 0, at Fenway Park

8

BEST YEARS ENJOYED BY RED SOX PITCHERS

H ow does one measure the best year for a starter? There are a number of metrics one could apply.

ERA

The Red Sox pitcher with the best earned run average in a given season has held the record for more than one hundred years. It was Dutch Leonard, with a 0.96 ERA in 1914. That's not just a Red Sox record; it's a major-league record. The next best on the list are as follows:

> *Cy Young. 1.26 in 1908*
> *Joe Wood. 1.49 in 1915*
> *Rip Collins. 1.62 in 1910*
> *Cy Young (again). 1.61 in 1901, the first year of the franchise*

While we're at it, what about career ERA? Among Red Sox pitchers who worked at least one thousand innings for the team, Joe Wood was tops here, the only one coming in under two runs a game per nine innings pitched. Wood's career ERA with the Boston Red Sox was 1.99. He just edged out Cy Young, at 2.00. We have to get to number seven on the list before we encounter a pitcher from modern times. Here is the ranking:

Joe Wood. 1.96
Cy Young. 2.00
Dutch Leonard. 2.13
Babe Ruth. 2.19
Carl Mays. 2,21
Rip Collins. 2.51
Pedro Martínez. 2.52
Roger Clemens comes in at number eleven, behind Bill Dinneen, George Winter, and Tex Hughson.

WINS/LOSSES

No one's likely to ever touch—or even approach—"Smoky" Joe Wood's 1912 season for winning percentage. That year, Wood was 34-5 (.872; he won more than 87 percent of his decisions that year). And he won a team-record 16 games in a row at one point. After winning 8 in a row, he lost on the Fourth of July. But starting with a win over St. Louis, he went on a tear, winning games on July 8, 12, 17, 23, and 28; August 2, 6, 10, 14, 20, 24, and 28; and September 2, 6, 10, and 15. And then he lost another game. In 1912, 16 of his wins were on the road; that's the most by any pitcher in team history. He also holds the record for the most wins at Fenway Park in a given season: 18. (In the pre-Fenway days, Cy Young won 19 home games at the Huntington Avenue Grounds in 1901.)

Let's pause for a moment and consider two other lengthy winning streaks.

The second-longest winning streak by a Red Sox pitcher was that executed by Roger Clemens in 1986. He started the season with a win on Opening Day, in Chicago. Including that game, he won on April 11, 17, 22, and 29; May 4, 14, 20, and 25; and June 6, 11, 16, 21, and 27. That's right. He didn't lose a game in all of April, May, and June. He was 14-0 heading into July. He got his comeuppance on July 2, 1982, when Toronto handed him a 4–2 loss at Fenway Park. Before the season was over, he had lost 3 more games, but he won another 10, for a final record of 24-4. The last game he lost was on August 4, and he didn't lose again the rest of the year.

Third on the list of consecutive win streaks is Ellis Kinder, with 13. The year was 1949, when he turned thirty-five years old. He was having a good season, 10-5 through July 24, when he lost a 9–8 game in relief. Then he reeled off a string of wins: July 28; August 3, 9, 13, 19, 26, and 30; and

September 3, 9, 14, and 18. The first 11 of the wins were—every one of them—a complete-game win. On September 21, Kinder worked the final three innings of a game against the visiting Cleveland Indians and won. On September 24, he shut out the Yankees in Boston, 3–0. That was the final win in the 13-game streak.

Returning to the matter of winning percentage, second on the list of starters is Rogelio Moret. He ranks right up there. More often considered a reliever, in fact, his 1973 season showed him at 13-2 (.867). And it wasn't just a fluky year. Just two years later, in 1975, he was 14-3 (.824), leading the major leagues that year. That was a mixed year; he actually started 16 games and relieved in 20 more; 10 of his 14 wins were in starts. In 1973, he was 50-50, or should we say 15-15, in terms of starts and relief gigs, but 12 of the 13 were as a starter.

Following Moret are two pitchers with the same .857 percentage: Roger Clemens (1986) and Daisuke Matsuzaka (2008). We just saw Roger Clemens a few paragraphs earlier, winning his first 14 games of 1986. By the end of the year, he was indeed 24-4. He was 0-0 in the 1986 World Series against the Mets, though. Clemens had started Game Two but was taken out after four and one-third innings with the Red Sox leading, 6–2. A runner he had left on base scored, but the Red Sox went on to win the game. He was two outs short of qualifying for a win. With the Red Sox leading the Series, three games to two, Clemens started the fateful Game Six. He worked seven innings, giving up just two runs (one unearned). When he left, the Red Sox were winning, 3–2. Reliever Calvin Schiraldi blew a save, and then his replacement, Bob Stanley, blew another save in the same game (after the Sox had scored two in the top of the tenth). Enough about that game.

Daisuke Matsuzaka matched Clemens's .857 winning percentage in 2008. In his rookie year with the Red Sox, he had won 15 games in the regular season, the decisive Game Seven in the American League Championship Series against the Indians and Game Three of the World Series against the Rockies. He had earned a ring. And he struck out 201 batters, shattering the previous Red Sox rookie record (155, by Ken Brett in 1970). In 2008, he helped the Red Sox reach the playoffs again, with an 18-3 record (thus, the .857 winning percentage), with a 2.90 ERA, and he pitched seven shutout innings to help the Red Sox win the first game of the ALCS against Tampa Bay. But Tampa Bay won the seven-game ALCS, and the Red Sox went home for the winter. "Dice-K" never had another particularly good year. He was 17-22 over his next four seasons with the Red Sox.

Pedro Martínez is next on the list, with his 23-4 (.852) season in 1999, followed by Rick Porcello (.846, 22-4 in 2016). Pedro pops up again with his 20-4 season in 2002, a .833 winning percentage.

See reliever Bob Stanley in chapter 12, however, for a reliever who posted an even better winning percentage in 1978.

Career winning percentage? Don't feel too sorry for Pedro Martínez, coming in behind Wood, Clemens, and Matsuzaka. For his Red Sox career, Pedro ranks number one. Among pitchers with 100 or more decisions during their Red Sox years, Pedro won 76 percent of them. He was 117-37 (.760). Joe Wood ranks second (116-56, 674). And guess who ranks third? Babe Ruth (89-46, a .659 Red Sox career winning percentage). Next up on the leader board are the following:

Tex Hughson. 96-54, .640
Jon Lester. 110-63, .636
Roger Clemens. 192-111, .634
Cy Young. 192-112, .632
Lefty Grove. 105-62, .629

9
SHUTOUTS

Of course, there are wins, and there are wins. An increasingly rare event is the shutout. A pitcher needs to work a complete game to be credited with a shutout. That simply doesn't happen as much in these days of strict pitch-count limits. The most shutouts any Red Sox pitcher threw in one season is 10. Two right-handers share that record: Cy Young in 1904 and Joe Wood in 1912. The left-hander with the most shutouts in a given season for the Red Sox is Babe Ruth, with 9 in 1916; Ruth is tied for this American League record. He started 41 games that year. He still holds the team record for the most starts by a left-handed pitcher. (Cy Young's 43 starts in 1902 is the overall team record for most starts.)

Earlier in the book, we saw some pitchers who threw a shutout in their debut game: Boo Ferriss, Lefty Hockette, Larry Pape, and Billy Rohr. There was also a pitcher who threw a shutout in his final game as a major leaguer: Brian Denman beat the Yankees, 5–0, on October 2, 1982.

It's one thing to win a 5–0 shutout but another to win one 1–0. As we have seen, Cy Young threw the longest shutout in team history, one that lasted fifteen innings and wound up a 1–0 victory on May 11, 1904. Remarkably, in the 1918 season, "Bullet" Joe Bush threw five 1–0 shutouts. In each case, he won the game with the barest amount of run support necessary. He beat the Yankees on April 23, the White Sox on May 28, the White Sox again (on the road) on June 10, the Indians on July 9 and the Tigers on July 22. Clearly, this Red Sox team wasn't scoring a ton of runs for him. In fact, he *lost* 1–0 shutouts on May 23, August 22 and August 31. And he was on the losing end of four other shutouts. Bush had an ERA that year of 2.11 but finished

Chris Sale long-tossing, 2019. *Bill Nowlin photo.*

the season 15-15. The one game he started in the World Series against the Cubs, he lost, 3–1.

Despite being a war-shortened season, with no regular-season games at all played in September, the 1918 Red Sox still set a record for the most shutouts by any Sox team: 26. In a 126-game season. Carl Mays had 8 of them, Joe Bush had 7, Sad Sam Jones have 5, Dutch Leonard had 3, and King Bader and Babe Ruth each had 1. One shutout required more than one pitcher, but it was still a shutout. Ruth also shut out the Cubs in Game One of the World Series, 1–0.

In all of 2018, there were zero shutouts. In fact, from May 27, 2017, to June 5, 2019—more than two calendar years—no Red Sox pitcher threw a complete-game shutout. Chris Sale threw one on the 2019 date, a three-hitter against the Royals. Sale's outing included an "immaculate" inning—nine pitches, nine strikes, three outs. It was his second such inning of the 2019 season.

Speaking of threes, there have been eleven seasons in which Red Sox pitchers threw 3 shutouts in a row. The most recent was in 2015, when they shut out the Baltimore Orioles for all three games of a visit. The O's came to Fenway and played games on September 25, 26, and 27 and then left, having not scored a single run over the weekend, losing 7–0, 8–0 and 2–0. They only mustered twelve base hits over the three games.

Rookie Dave Ferriss shut out the opposition five times in 1945.

Of course, the Red Sox do get shut out sometimes, too. Sox fans like it better when they are not. There was a nice stretch in 1950 when no opposing team shut out the Sox for 136 games, all the way after April 24 until September 23.

10

WHIP AND WAR

Two more recently developed statistics attempt to measure the effectiveness of a pitcher relative to others. They are WHIP (Walks and Hits per Inning Pitched) and WAR (Wins above Replacement.)

WHIP

Let's look at WHIP first and then WAR. Unlike WAR, WHIP is a precise calculation. As explained in a glossary on the MLB.com site:

WHIP is, as Major League Baseball explains:

> *One of the most commonly used statistics for evaluating a pitcher's performance. The statistic shows how well a pitcher has kept runners off the basepaths, one of his main goals. The formula is simple enough—it's the sum of a pitcher's walks and hits, divided by his total innings pitched.*
>
> *The pitchers with the lowest WHIPs are generally the best pitchers in the league—which makes sense, because the best pitchers should be able to prevent baserunners. However, WHIP does not consider the way in which a hitter reached base. (Obviously, home runs are more harmful to pitchers than walks.)*
>
> *Hit batsmen, errors and hitters who reach via fielder's choice do not count against a pitcher's WHIP.*[7]

A WHIP of 1.00 would thus mean that a pitcher had allowed an average of one batter per inning to reach base via hit or base on balls. In one sense, that might seem like a lot—nine baserunners per game. As suggested, if the nine baserunners had all hit solo home runs, the pitcher would have yielded nine runs and it would be deemed a dismal performance. That has never happened. But in fact, pitching is difficult, and a WHIP of 1.00 ranks very high.

The Top 10 Single-Season WHIP Rankings for Red Sox Pitchers

1. Pedro Martínez (2000, 0.7373)

In this season, Red Sox right-hander Pedro Martínez recorded the best WHIP of any pitcher in all of baseball history. Yes, Pedro ranks number one of all time. His WHIP for the season was .7373. He threw 217 innings, allowing 32 walks and 128 base hits. Following the formula, add 32 to 128 (160) and divide by 217. That comes to .7373271. As one might expect, other stats fall in line: in 2000, Pedro's 1.74 earned run average led both leagues—by almost two full runs. Second that year in the American League was Roger Clemens with a 3.70 ERA. In the National League, the Dodgers' Kevin Brown had a 2.58 ERA.

Pedro averaged 11.8 strikeouts per nine innings (he struck out 284 batters in 217 innings) and walked only 32 batters all year in 29 starts.

2. Cy Young (1905, .8669)

We shall see the names of Pedro Martínez and Cy Young appear numerous times on this list. They were both that good. Young's second-place all-time team ranking was his 1905 season. This was one of six seasons, all between 1901 and 1908, in which he posted a WHIP below 1.0. He worked 320⅔ innings, allowing 248 base hits but only walking thirty batters all season long. The team finished fourth (78-75), and Young himself had a losing season (18-19) despite a 1.82 earned run average. As far as wins go, the only pitcher with more than 3 wins and a winning record was left-hander Jesse Tannehill, who was 22-9. His ERA was 2.48 and his WHIP was 1.093. So, Young pitched superbly but didn't get the wins. His 7.3 WAR was best on the team and topped Tannehill's 6.1. Note: See comments regarding Chris Sale later in this list. Sale's 2018 season would rank number two on this list if Baseball-Reference.com's threshold was set to match Major League Baseball's.

3. Dutch Leonard (1914, .8800)

Hubert Benjamin "Dutch" Leonard had a sophomore season par excellence. As noted earlier, he recorded the best earned run average in the history of baseball, 0.96, in a season in which he pitched in 36 games (28 starts) and was 19-5. He worked 224⅔ innings. Leonard gave up 139 hits and walked 60. He struck out 176 batters. In his six seasons pitching for the Red Sox (1913–18), the *worst* ERA he ever recorded was 2.72, in 1918. Is that why he was traded to the Yankees? New York sold his contract to the Tigers before he pitched for the Yanks. For the Red Sox, Leonard was 1-0 in the five-game 1915 World Series (a complete-game 2–1 victory) and 1-0 in the five-game 1916 World Series (a 6–2 complete game, in which only one of the two runs was earned.) His World Series ERA was thus 1.00 both years.

4. Cy Young (1908, .8930)

Here we encounter Cy Young again. He ranks both second and fourth on the list (and seventh and ninth). His 1908 season saw him wearing a Red Sox uniform, not a Boston Americans one. It was his sixteenth (and last) 20-win season. He had five 30-win seasons. In 1908, he was 21-11 with a stingy 1.26 earned run average. He worked 299 innings, with 230 base hits and 37 walks.

Pedro Martinez taking batting practice before a set of interleague games, June 2004. *Bill Nowlin photo.*

5. Pedro Martínez (2002, .9231)

After outstanding seasons in 1999 and 2000, Pedro had an off year in 2001, due to a rotator cuff injury, but he bounced back big time in 2002. His won-loss record was 20-4 with a major-league-leading ERA of 2.26. He pitched 199⅓ innings, allowing 144 hits and 40 walks. His 239 strikeouts led the league. Martínez came in second only to Barry Zito in the Cy Young Award voting.

6. Pedro Martínez (1999, .9234)

In his final year with the Montreal Expos (1997), Pedro recorded a WHIP of .9323. Red Sox GM Dan Duquette was well aware of Pedro's greatness and did what he needed to do to bring him to Boston. After the 2004 season, Duquette elected not to pursue Pedro as hard as he might have when Pedro elected free agency, and one could argue that the record bears out his decision. In his first year with the New York Mets (2005), Pedro recorded a .9493 WHIP, good enough to lead both leagues. But over his final four years in the majors, Pedro Martínez won a total of just 22 games. His career WHIP was 1.054, an indication of just how extraordinary it is to have a WHIP under 1.000. In Pedro's 1999 season, his WHIP of .9234 was reflected in his 23-4 record and his 2.07 ERA. He struck out 313 and walked only 37.

7. Cy Young (1904, .9365)
Here's Cy Young again. Boston won the American League pennant for the second year in a row. They had won the first World Series in 1903, and the National League's New York Giants refused to play them in 1904. The World Series became a truly annual event the next year, 1905. Had John McGraw's Giants faced the Boston Americans, they would have had to face Cy Young (26-16, 1.97). He started 41 games and relieved in 2 others. Of his 41 starts, 40 resulted in complete games; 10 were shutouts. He allowed 327 base hits, but he had worked a staggering 380 innings. He walked 29 batters.

8. Roger Clemens (1986, .9685)
The Red Sox won the pennant in 1986. This was the year the "Rocket" won his first 14 decisions and finished 24-4, with an ERA of 2.48. It was also the year he recorded his first 20-strikeout game and the year in which he won both the Most Valuable Player Award and the first of his seven Cy Young Awards—three were with the Red Sox (1986, 1997, and 1991). He pitched 33 games (10 complete), working 254 innings. He allowed 179 hits and 67 BBs.

9. Cy Young (1903, .9688)
This was the year the first World Series was played. Young started and lost the first World Series game, Game One, 7–3 (only three of the Pirate runs were earned). He won Game Five (11–2, no earned runs) and Game Seven (7–3, all three runs earned.) The regular season is what his WHIP is based on. He was 28-9 (2.08). In 341⅔ innings, he walked 37 and allowed 294 hits. His seven shutouts led both leagues.

10. Chris Sale (2017, .9705)
The most recent pitcher on the list is Chris Sale, working in his first season with the Red Sox. As he is still pitching for the Red Sox as this book is

being written, we can't know how his career will unfold, but we can look back and see that he has put up some special stats for the Sox—the White Sox, where he began his career, and the Red Sox from 2017. In fact, his .861 WHIP for the 2018 regular season would rank him second on this list. One presumes that BR.com left him off its list because the 158 innings he worked fell below a threshold of qualifiers; he fell just 4 innings short of 162, which would be 1 inning pitched for every game the team played. That would have qualified him. He was good enough, though, to qualify in the Cy Young voting, placing fourth. Leaving 2018 aside, however, in 2017, Sale worked 214⅓ innings, walking 43 (but striking out a major-league-leading 308) and allowing 165 base hits. As of the end of the 2019 season, his 11.1 strikeouts per nine innings pitched ranks him tops among all major-league pitchers of all time. His strikeout-to-walk ratio of 5.37 is also the all-time career record.

Number 11 on the Red Sox list is…Cy Young yet again (.9722 in 1901, the first year of the franchise.)

Number 12 is Derek Lowe, with a .9742 WHIP in 2002.

WAR

WAR is more complicated and less precise. It is explained on the Fangraphs site thus:

> *Wins Above Replacement (WAR) is an attempt by the sabermetric baseball community to summarize a player's total contributions to their team in one statistic. You should always use more than one metric at a time when evaluating players, but WAR is all-inclusive and provides a useful reference point for comparing players. WAR offers an estimate to answer the question, "If this player got injured and their team had to replace them with a freely available minor leaguer or a AAAA player from their bench, how much value would the team be losing?" This value is expressed in a wins format, so we could say that Player X is worth +6.3 wins to their team while Player Y is only worth +3.5 wins, which means it is highly likely that Player X has been more valuable than Player Y.*[8]

Top 10 Single-Season WAR Rankings for Red Sox Pitchers

1. Cy Young (1901, 12.6)

He may be number 11 with WHIP, but in Wins above Replacement, Cy Young is number 1. This ranking poses Young's contribution to this season as being the biggest contribution that any pitcher in the 119-year history of the franchise (through 2019) has made toward the success of the team in that particular season. In its very first season, the Bostons finished in second place, four games behind the Chicago White Sox. Their record was 79-57. Cy Young's record was 33-10. He won more than 41 percent of the team's wins for the season. The number 2 and number 3 pitchers on the team—Ted Lewis and George Winter—each won 16 games, so we can see that Cy won more than the two of them added together. They lost 29 games; he lost 10. His 1.62 earned run average was (as with his number of wins) the best in both leagues. Had there been a Cy Young Award, he would have won it.

2. Pedro Martínez (2000, 11.7)

Pedro did have the number 1 WHIP among all Red Sox pitchers, all-time—in fact, of any major-league pitcher, ever. We needn't recite again all the statistics cited just a few pages earlier, but we will emphasize again how dominant he was in the league, his 1.74 ERA being just shy of 2 runs better than any other pitcher in the league in 2000. He was 18-6; no other pitcher on the Red Sox staff won more than 10 games (that was Pedro's older brother Ramon Martínez). Rich Garces and Jeff Fassero each won eight. Statistically asserted, Pedro's contribution to the Red Sox second-place finish, 2½ games behind the Yankees, was bigger than any contribution any pitcher other than Cy Young in 1901 had made to a franchise team.

3. Smoky Joe Wood (1912, 11.4)

His overall player WAR is presented here, not just his WAR as a pitcher. WAR can be calculated separately for his pitching stats, and Baseball-Reference has Wood's WAR as a pitcher at 10.1. He'd still make the top 10 with ease. But, of course, Joe Wood was more than just a pitcher. He played sixty years before the designated hitter became part of American League play. In 1912, he pitched in 43 games. But he came to bat more than three times per game (3.28), with 141 plate appearances. He hit for a .290 average (the overall team batting average was .277 in 1912) and achieved a .348 on-base percentage. He drove in 13 runs and scored 16. This was the year Wood posted a 34-5 record, throwing 10 shutouts and ending the season with a 1.91 ERA. In the World Series, he won three of the four games that gave the Red Sox bragging rights as champions of the world in 1912. His World Series work is not included in the WAR calculation, but to have accounted for more than 11 wins above a replacement player ranked him the top player on the team, above Tris Speaker's 10.1.

4. Lefty Grove (1936, 10.7)

Lefty Grove is in the National Baseball Hall of Fame largely for his work for Connie Mack's Philadelphia Athletics. He was 195-79 for the A's. That work (1925–33) included seven 20-win seasons, one of them a 31-win season. For the Red Sox, he was 105-62. In 1935, he was 20-12; in 1937, he was 17-9. One might think either of those seasons was a better one than his 1936 season, when he was 17-12. But it's all relative. His 2.81 ERA for the 1936 Red Sox team led the league; no one on the whole team posted any better than Wes Ferrell's 4.19. The team had a losing season, 74-80.

5. Wes Ferrell (1935, 10.6)

As with Joe Wood, Wes Ferrell's best single-season WAR as a player was distinctly higher than his WAR as a pitcher, which was 8.2. Second on the 1935 team was Lefty Grove (8.6). The highest any nonpitcher ranked was, interestingly, Rick Ferrell (3.7). Rick, a catcher, was Wes's brother (and sometimes batterymate). Wes was 25-14 in 1935, leading the league in wins. He threw a major-league-leading 31 complete games. One of the reasons

Brothers Rick (*seated*) and Wes Ferrell (*with bat*). Rick's in the Hall of Fame, but the brother who was arguably better is not. *Leslie Jones photograph, Boston Public Library.*

Wes ranked so high was his skill as a batter. He hit for a .347 batting average in 1935, with 7 homers and 32 RBIs. The RBI leader on the '35 Red Sox was Joe Cronin, with 95, but no one else on the team drove in more than 66. The 32 RBIs are, by far, the most ever driven in by a Red Sox pitcher. Ranking second is Wes Ferrell with 24 in 1936, and third is Babe Ruth with 21 in 1915. Ferrell was such a good batter than he was used as a pinch-hitter thirty-five times during the course of the season. On back-to-back days, July 21 and 22, he hit walk-off home runs to win the games.

6. Roger Clemens (1990, 10.4)
It may be a surprise that Roger Clemens's highest-ranked year for WAR was not one of his three Cy Young Award–winning seasons for the Red Sox. He did come in second, though, in 1990, behind 27-game winner Bob Welch's anomalous season. Clemens's record was 21-6. His 1.93 ERA led the majors. The Red Sox finished first in the standings. Mike Boddicker was second on the Sox at 17-8 (3.36).

7. Lefty Grove (1937, 9.8)
Grove was 17-9 in 1937. He had a 3.02 ERA, not far off his career ERA of 3.06. Lifetime, he was 300-141 (a career winning percentage of .680). But in 1937, his winning percentage was a below-average (for him) .654. In 1937, though, his 3.02 ERA was much better than his team's 4.48. There were few other players who approached him on the team: fellow pitcher Jack Wilson's WAR was 5.3, and shortstop/manager Joe Cronin's WAR was 3.7.

8. Pedro Martínez (1999, 9.8)
In the WHIP section, we saw that Pedro's 1999 season ranks sixth. His 1999 season ranks eighth in WAR. We can expect that, with baseline stats such as his 23-4 record (led the majors in wins and in win-loss percentage), his 2.07 ERA (led the majors), and his 313 strikeouts (led the majors and remains the all-time Red Sox record), he'd be included in this top 10 list. And, indeed, here he is. He earned it. There were 19 games in which he struck out 10 or more batters, including one stretch of 7 early on and one stretch of 8 10-K games later in the season.

9. Cy Young (1902, 9.7)
Cy Young ranks first, as we have seen, with his 1901 season. The very next year, he earned himself another slot in the top 10. His won-loss record was 32-11. Not too shabby, as the saying goes. His earned run average was 2.15—

excellent by any standard but remarkable in that it was the *worst* ERA he recorded in the first five years of the franchise. His ERAs were, in sequence: 1.62, 2.15, 2.08, 1.97, and 1.82. He totally fell apart with a 3.19 in 1906 (most Cy Young Award contenders today would be pleased with a 3.19) but then came back with 1.99 in 1907 and then the best of his career, 1.26, in 1908. An ERA is only part of the equation. He won 32 of the team's 77 victories in 1902 and threw 41 complete games.

10. Roger Clemens (1987, 9.4)

Roger Clemens often completed games, too. In 1987, he worked a majors-leading 18 complete games; 7 of them were shutouts. That led both leagues. His record was 20-9; the 20 wins was also better than anyone else in either league. He received 21 of the 28 first-place votes for the Cy Young Award and earned his second in succession.

So, TO TRY AND select the single best season any Sox pitcher ever had, let's recap a bit.

Pedro Martínez (2000)

What had Pedro Martínez done in 1999? He won the Cy Young Award and was the MVP of the All-Star Game (held at Fenway Park). The *Sporting News* named him American League Pitcher of the Year. He struck out 313, still the Red Sox single-season record. He was 23-4—in case wins matter to you (they sure matter to everyone else). It was the best record in baseball, as was his 2.07 earned run average. Could he be any better? Yes, in the very next year. OK, he didn't win as many games, but his ERA was 1.74 (the league average was 4.91). His WHIP (Walks and Hits per Inning Pitched) was .737; in 1999, it had been .923. His strikeout-to-walks ratio was 8.88 (better than the 8.46 in 1999). Martínez allowed opposing batters to hit just .167 off him, the stingiest performance by any major-league pitcher since such records began to be kept in the 1800s. His On-Base Percentage Against average was .213, the lowest since 1884. And it's pretty hard to compare baseball in 1884 to baseball more than one hundred years later. For the second year in a row, he was the unanimous choice for the Cy Young Award.

ASIDE FROM THE QUANTITATIVE approach, using various statistically based measures, there is another way of looking at the question. Rather than asking how to measure the best year for a pitcher, one might ask how to assess the best year for a pitcher. Here is one nomination to consider, for what one might argue was the best year a pitcher could hope to have.

Derek Lowe (2004)

Lowe pitched eight seasons for the Boston Red Sox. Statistically, his best year was 2002, when he was 21-8 with a 2.58 ERA. The 21 wins were his career high, and his .724 winning percentage that year was his best. Pedro Martínez that year, though, was 20-4 (.833) with a 2.26 ERA. Pedro had a better year. Barry Zito won the Cy Young Award. Pedro placed second, and Lowe placed third. In 2004, Lowe's record wasn't at all spectacular. He was 14-2 with a 5.42 ERA in a year when the team ERA was 4.18. It was not a particularly good year, but Lowe got to enjoy something that had eluded every Red Sox pitcher for the prior eighty-six years. He was on the first Red Sox World Champion team since 1918. The 2002 team hadn't even made the postseason.

Derek Lowe did something in 2004 that has never been done before or since, by any pitcher. He won the deciding game in each round of the playoffs. It was his "W" that clinched the American League Division Series, the American League Championship Series, and the World Series. Could you ask for a better way to finish a season?

The Red Sox won the first two games of the best-of-three ALDS against the Angels. It was a game at Fenway Park, and the Red Sox were leading, 5–1, after six innings. Things were looking fine. In the top of the seventh, though, a bases-loaded walk and a grand slam by Vladimir Guerrero sobered up the crowd pretty quickly. The game was tied. It went into extra innings, and Lowe was asked to work the top of the tenth. There was a walk and a single but no run scored. In the bottom of the tenth, with two outs and pinch-runner Pokey Reese on base, David Ortiz homered and won the game, 8–6. The win landed in Lowe's lap.

In the ALCS against the Yankees, Lowe started Game Four. He worked into the sixth, leaving the game with a 3–2 lead but a runner on third base. That inherited runner scored. The Red Sox won, much later, in the twelfth, thanks to Ortiz homering again. Lowe was long gone. But he also started Game Seven. The Red Sox had miraculously come back from losing the first three games with three wins of their own. Game Seven, of course, was for the American League pennant. Lowe started and threw six innings of one-hit baseball. In the meantime, the Red Sox scored twice in the first (Ortiz home run) and four times in the second (Johnny Damon grand slam).

Yankee Stadium was pretty somber. After six and a half innings, it was Red Sox 8, Yankees 1 when the New Yorkers came up to bat in the bottom of the seventh. Who came on in relief for the Red Sox? Pedro Martínez! He gave up a couple of runs. The Red Sox got another couple of runs. The final was 10–3, Sox. And Lowe got the W.

Lowe was equally superb in Game Four of the 2004 World Series against St. Louis. The Red Sox swept, and it was Lowe, working seven full innings, who kept the Cardinals scoreless and with just three base hits. The bullpen took over; they didn't allow any runs, either. There were two outs in the bottom of the ninth, and then the famous Joe Castiglione commentary: "Swing and a ground ball stabbed by Foulke. He has it. He underhands to first and the Boston Red Sox are the World Champions. For the first time in eighty-six years the Red Sox have won baseball's World Championship. Can you believe it!"

How can you top that?

11

SOME PITCHING MISCELLANY

WINS IN BACK-TO-BACK SEASONS

We have seen that Smoky Joe Wood won 34 games in 1912. He had won 23 the year before, for a total of 57 in back-to-back seasons. The back-to-back record for the franchise is held by Cy Young (65), with 33 wins in 1901 and 32 wins in 1902. So, OK, Cy Young is first with 65 and Joe Wood ranks second with 57. Who's third on the list? It wasn't Roger Clemens, with 24 wins in 1986 and 20 in 1987—that totals "only" 44. Mel Parnell (1949), Boo Ferriss (1946), and Wes Ferrell (1935) each had 25-win seasons. But Parnell won 15 the year before and 18 the year after, so his best back-to-back total is 43. For Ferriss, his best adjacent year was 1945, when he won 21. That's a very good back-to-back total of 46. Wes Ferrell was a 20-game winner in 1936, so his total comes to 45. Who's the best since Joe Wood? You guessed it. Babe Ruth. He won 23 games in 1916 and then 24 in 1917, for a total of 47. Really, you guessed that? Very good for you!

THE WORST YEAR EVER?

For the worst year a Red Sox starter ever bore (*enjoyed* is hardly the word that one would apply), see the case of Joe Harris, detailed later in this book.

20-GAME LOSERS ON THE RED SOX

In the history of major-league baseball, there have been 499 pitchers who had seasons in which they lost 20 or more games.[9] That list even includes several Hall of Famers, including two who pitched for the Red Sox. Most of these 20-game losing seasons happened almost one hundred years ago. For the Red Sox, there hasn't been a 20-game loser since 1930. Here is the list, in chronological order, of 20-game losers on the Red Sox.

1. Bill Dinneen (1902, 21-21)
A 20-game winner and a 20-game loser, both in the same season!

2. Cy Young (1906, 13-21)
The great Cy Young was a three-time 20-game loser, but he experienced this misfortune just this one time for Boston.

3. Joe Harris (1906, 2-21)
See chapter 31.

4. "Sad" Sam Jones (1919, 12-20)
"Something is happening and you don't know what it is, do you, Mr. Jones?" It's safe to assume it made him sad to make such a list. Two years later, he recorded a 23-16 season for the Red Sox. Dealt to the Yankees, he had a 21-win season for them in 1922 and a 21-loss season in 1925.

5. Howard Ehmke (1925, 9-20)
Yes, Ehmke was pitching for a really poor team (the Red Sox were 47-105 in 1925), but how is it that Ehmke lost more than twice as many games as he won but still ranked in the MVP voting? Yes, he ranked just twenty-fourth, but that had him tied with Lou Gehrig. His ERA was 3.73. He did lead the American League with 22 complete games.

6. "Slim" Harriss (1927, 14-21)
William Jennings Bryan Harriss matched Ehmke in one regard. Despite being a 20-game loser (for the second time in his career; see 1922 with the Philadelphia Athletics), he also ranked in MVP voting. In Slim's case, and despite a 4.18 ERA, he was number 25. Oddly, five of the top 25 were Red Sox players…on a team that lost 101 games!

7. Red Ruffing (1928, 10-25)

Like Cy Young, Red Ruffing also became a Hall of Famer. He was 39-96 for the Red Sox during the worst decade in team history. With an 0-3 record, he was traded/sold to the Yankees in May 1930. For them he was 15-5 and, ultimately, 231-124.

8. Red Ruffing (1929, 9-22)

Two years in a row, Ruffing earned the distinction.

9. Jack Russell (1930, 9-20)

This right-hander had seven seasons under his belt before he had a winning season (for Washington in 1933). All those losses had a lot to do with playing for that era's Red Sox, though his 5.45 ERA in 1930 certainly wasn't all that intimidating.

10. Milt Gaston (1930, 13-20)

Two 20-game losers in the same season, just like in 1906. Suffice it to say, neither was a very good season for the team. One wonders whether, if they had kept Ruffing, they could have pulled off a true trifecta: three 20-game losers. The 1930 team lost 97 games; there were plenty of losses to be shared. Hod Lisenbee lost 17, and Ed Durham lost 15. Neither is celebrated in Red Sox lore.

12

A SPECIAL SECTION ON RELIEF PITCHERS

Over the years, relief pitching has become an increasingly important part of the game. Notions of starters pitching complete games are part of the past. It's astonishing to look at a season such as 1904 and see that the team's starters that year pitched 148 complete games—in a season shorter than today's 162-game schedule. Boston was 95-59, with three tie games. With today's emphasis on pitch count, we've even seen a pitcher with a clear shot at setting the major-league record for strikeouts (Chris Sale on May 24, 2019) being removed from the game because he had thrown 108 pitches and the manager feared taxing his very valuable arm. The 17 Ks that Sale recorded in the seven innings he pitched set a major-league record.

As a side note to the same year of 1904, Cy Young walked just 29 batters all season, despite throwing 380 innings. That had him well under 1 walk per game (he appeared in 43 games that year, 41 of them starts); it was a major-league record until the Twins' Carlos Silva edged out Cy in 2005 with 0.4 walks per nine innings.

Now let's look at ERA and winning percentage for Red Sox relievers.

ERA

On the list of Red Sox pitchers, no reliever even cracks the top 10 in ERA. With a minimum of one thousand innings in a Red Sox uniform, the top reliever in career earned run average is Ellis Kinder. His 3.28 Red Sox career ERA places him twelfth on the list.

Relief could be just a phone call away. Fenway Park dugout phone to the bullpen. *Bill Nowlin photo.*

We have to drop all the way to number 20 before we encounter another Red Sox reliever. That was Bob Stanley, at 3.64. That's not to say that all of the appearances by the "Steamer" were in relief roles. He pitched for the Red Sox from 1977 through 1989—thirteen seasons—and played for no other big-league team. Among his 637 appearances were 85 starts, 30 of them in 1979 alone. But he was first and foremost a relief pitcher.

Stanley holds the team record for the most innings thrown by a relief pitcher in a given season, 168⅓, in 1982. It is an American League record, too. Only two starters worked more innings: Dennis Eckersley (224⅓) and John Tudor (195⅔). Both won 13 games. Stanley appeared in 48 games, all in relief, closing 33 of them. He had a record of 12-7 and was credited with 14 saves. His ERA was 3.10 that year.

Bob Stanley also holds the team record for the most career wins by a relief pitcher: 82. Dick Radatz had 49, and Ellis Kinder had 41. Chances are that almost no one (other than perhaps a relative) would guess who ranks fourth on the list: Mark Clear, with 35. It's true. Despite a 4.27 ERA over five seasons with the Red Sox, and never a start, we verified it: 1981 (803), 1982 (14-9), 1983 (4-5), 1984 (8-30), and 1985 (1-3).

WINS-LOSSES

With a minimum of 15 decisions in a given year (which is admittedly maybe a little high for a relief pitcher), the best season any Red Sox pitcher (including starters) ever had in terms of win-loss percentage is held by Bob Stanley. In 1978, he was 15-2 (.882). He appeared in 48 games but without a single start that season. His winning percentage that season was better than any achieved by Smoky Joe, the Rocket, Dice-K, or Pedro.

Over the course of a career, though, the best relief record by one of the team's pitchers is the 24-4 (.857) held by Charley "Sea Lion" Hall (1909–13). Carlos Luis Hall was one of the first Latinos on the team.

A later Latino was Rich "El Guapo" Garces. His won-loss record with the Red Sox, after appearing in 261 games for Boston, was second only to Hall in terms of winning percentage: 23-8 (.742)

In more recent years, relievers who truly stand out include Dick Radatz, Koji Uehara, and Craig Kimbrel. We could have named quite a few more but will settle on these three. Radatz (the "Monster") may have been ridden a little too hard, called on a little too often. In 1963, he was 15-6 (an extraordinary number of decisions for a relief pitcher) with a 1.97 ERA, and in 1964, he was 16-9 (2.29). He struck out 181 batters in the latter year, still the team record for a relief pitcher. Not only did he win 16 games; he also saved a major-league-leading 29 games. His weren't brief appearances. He averaged close to two full innings per appearance.

Koji Uehara joined the Red Sox as a free agent in December 2012. He earned a World Championship ring in 2013 with a 4-1 record in a team-leading 73 appearances. His ERA was a miniscule 1.09. He was the eighth-inning guy at the start of the season, but on June 26, he became the closer. From that point on, he gave up a total of 2 earned runs, one on June 30 and one on September 17. (You can look it up.) That's all. Just 2 earned runs (and only 1 unearned run) in 41 appearances.

Koji holds the team record for the most consecutive batters retired by a reliever: 37, in 2013. On August 17, pitching the top of the ninth against the Yankees, he struck out the first two batters, gave up a double, and then induced a popup to third base. On August 18, he faced the Giants in the ninth and retired the side 1-2-3. Three days later, he faced 4 Dodgers and retired them all. On August 28: 3 Orioles batters and three outs. On August 30, he got all 4 White Sox batters he faced. On September 1, 3, 5, and 6, Koji faced 3 batters each game, and every one of them made outs. At this point, he had retired 27 consecutive batters without giving up a base hit or a walk, hitting a batter, or seeing a runner reach base on an error. In other words, he had pitched the equivalent of a perfect game. He wasn't done yet. On September 10, with the Red Sox holding a precarious 2–0 lead, Koji set down the 4 Rays he faced. The very next day, he worked the ninth again, getting three more outs and seeing the game head into extra innings. The Sox scored four runs in the top of the tenth, so they brought in Junichi Tazawa to end the game. As the pitcher of record, Koji got the win and became 4-0 on the season. On September 13, the Yankees were in Boston; Koji faced the last three batters and got all three. He had now retired 37 batters in a row—a perfect game plus 10 more batters. One month to the day from the start of his streak, it ended. It was September 17 in Boston. The first Oriole he faced tripled. He got the next three, but the first one was a sacrifice fly, driving in the baserunner from third. The Orioles won the game, 3–2, and Koji took the loss. He gave up three more hits before the end of the year (he didn't walk anyone). He finished the season with that 1.09 earned run average.

Uehara also holds the record for the most consecutive relief appearances without giving up a run: 27, also in 2013. It embraced the same stretch but started earlier. On July 6, he blew a save, giving up a run. The next 10 games he worked in July were all clean—no runs (earned or unearned). In August, he relieved in 10 games. Not once did the other team score on him. The same was true for the first 7 games he worked in September. Then came the September 17 triple and sacrifice fly. After July 6 and through September 16, some 72 calendar days had passed without anyone scoring a run off Koji Uehara, despite him working in 27 games.

Koji appeared in five of the six games of the American League Championship Series against the Detroit Tigers without giving up a run. He had saves in Games Three, Four, and Five. He was named the MVP of the ALCS. He also appeared in five games of the six-game World Series. Again, he didn't give up a run. And he earned saves in Games Four and Five. As Game Six unfolded, the Red Sox held a 6-1 lead after eight innings. Uehara came in to pitch the top of the ninth. Fly ball to left. Fly ball to left. And then a strikeout swinging for the final out of the World Series. The Red Sox had won the World Series on the field at Fenway Park for the first time since

An information kiosk at Fenway Park. *Bill Nowlin photo.*

1918. The 2004 and 2007 wins had both been on the road. Koji Uehara had thrown the final pitch of the year.

Craig Kimbrel's best year for the Red Sox was 2017. In sixty-seven appearances, he was 5-0 with a 1.43 earned run average. In sixty-nine innings, he struck out 126 opposing batters and walked just 14, a very impressive 9:1 strikeout-to-walk ratio. Over the full course of his career, which included work for the Braves and the Padres, Kimbrel had struck out batters at a rate of 14.7 per nine innings. In his three seasons with the Red Sox, he faced a total of 721 batters and struck out 305 of them.

Speaking of Bill Dinneen (which we were a few pages ago), he pops up in an unusual way when one thinks of relief pitchers and the role they play. In 1904, he started 37 games and threw 37 complete games. In other words, never once all season did he depart from the mound to be replaced by a reliever; not the time he gave up eight runs in the game, and not times he was leading by a big margin and could afford to sit out the last couple of innings. By no means did he win all 37 games; he lost 14 of them. (He was 23-14, every appearance resulting in a decision, since no one else beside him pitched for Boston on those days.) But his overall ERA was an excellent 2.20. He pitched 335⅔ innings that year—all without relief. Among his games were six extra-inning contests. The June 12 game ran sixteen innings. He won it, 2–1. His streak was longer than just the one season. He had finished 1903 with three complete games. (Dinneen also threw four complete games in the 1903 World Series—the first World Series in history—and was 3-1. Without a reliever.)

And he started 1905 with a complete-game, 11-inning win but was relieved in the seventh inning of the game on April 25, 1905. Adding in the 1903 innings, all of 1904 and the first 17 innings of 1905, Dinneen worked a total of 440⅔ consecutive innings before he left a game. If one wanted to toss in the 35 innings of World Series play—and why not, while we're at it—one finds that Dinneen worked 475⅔ innings, the equivalent of 52-plus 9-inning games between times a reliever was called on.

Pitchers like Bill Dinneen would have put a Dick Radatz out of work.

Keith Foulke was brought to the Red Sox for the 2004 season to do precisely what he did: close games. The 2003 Red Sox famously lost Game Seven of the ALCS after manager Grady Little tried to eke one more inning from Pedro Martínez. That didn't end well.

After arriving from the Arizona Diamondbacks in time to get into the June 1 game, Byung-Hyun Kim had been the closer in 2003. He'd been OK statistically for the Red Sox, but they had lost confidence in him and barely used him in the postseason. GM Theo Epstein signed Foulke as a free agent in early January 2004. Foulke worked in 72 games that year, closing 61 of them, and worked to a 2.17 earned run average. He was credited with 32 saves. In the postseason, he couldn't have been much better. He worked in Games Two and Three in the American League Division Series, with a save in Game Two. His ERA was 0.00. He worked in five of the seven ALCS games, again without giving up even one run. He earned a save in Game Six. In the 2004 World Series, two tying runs scored (both on unearned runs) in Game One, but Mark Bellhorn hit a two-run homer in the bottom of the eighth and Foulke picked up a win by holding the Cardinals scoreless in the ninth. He also closed Games Two, Three, and Four—in other words, every game—and earned a save in Game Four, a 3–0 win. He threw the final pitch (resulting in the famous "swing and a groundball stabbed by Foulke...").

MOST GAMES IN A SEASON

The pitcher who appeared in the most games during one season was right-handed reliever Mike Timlin. (You knew it wasn't going to be a starter.) In the 2005 season, Timlin appeared in 81 games. The math is fairly elementary: the Red Sox play a 162-game season. Timlin appeared in precisely 50 percent of the team's games. And he did so while being stingy with runs: his ERA for the year was 2.24.

In 2003, he appeared in 72 games (plus eight postseason games). In 2004, he appeared in 76 games (plus 11 postseason games). He only got into one postseason game in 2005; the Red Sox just didn't get very far. If one adds in the postseason games, the 87 he worked in 2004 was his career high—

and a Red Sox record. His regular season ERA was quite a bit higher than in 2005, however. It was 4.13. (The team ERA was 4.18 that year.) His postseason ERA was pretty high, but he bought the team innings and—what really matters—the Red Sox won the World Series for the first time in eighty-six years. Over six seasons, Timlin worked in 394 games for the Red Sox and 28 postseason games. He was 30-22 in the regular season (3.76). In the postseason, he was 0-1, with one blown save, a game the Red Sox came back and won (that would be the famous Game Four of the 2004 ALCS), but he had eight holds.

Some may wonder: who worked the most games as a left-handed pitcher for the Red Sox? The answer is: Rob Murphy, 74 (1989). Murphy pitched two seasons for the Red Sox, 1989 and 1990. He came over in

Mike Timlin averaged more than sixty-five relief appearances a year for the Red Sox. *Bill Nowlin photo.*

a trade from the Cincinnati Reds. He'd worked in 87 games for the Reds in 1987. The Red Sox were 83-79 in 1989, finishing in third place. Murphy pitched very well; his 2.74 ERA was bettered only by Dennis Lamp's 2.32. Lamp appeared in 42 games. Of Murphy's 74 games, he finished 27 of them. He threw 105 innings. His record was 5-7. In 1990, he was used in 68 games but was distinctly less effective: a 6.32 ERA and a won-loss record of 0-6 (in a year when the Red Sox finished in first place.)

MOST GAMES FINISHED

Tom Gordon was the closer in 1998. He appeared in 73 games, closing all but 4 of them. Thus, he finished 69 games. That led the American League. He booked 46 saves, also leading the league. The Red Sox won 92 games that year. Hence, Gordon earned a save in exactly 50 percent of the team's wins. In case you were wondering, there were five complete games that year. Dennis Eckersley and John Wasdin each finished 13 games. Rich Garces finished 11.

SAVES

Tom Gordon turns up again, looking at saves. Those 46 saves in 1998 remain the Red Sox team record. Second in the number of saves in a season are two pitchers with 42 apiece: Derek Lowe in 2000 and Craig Kimbrel in 2018. Jonathan Papelbon saved 41 games in 2008.

Tom Gordon also holds another team record regarding saves—most consecutive saves in a season: 43 in 1998. That's a deceptive stat, though. In 1998, he saved 3 games at the start of the season, but on April 14, he blew a save but won the game when Nomar Garciaparra hit a three-run homer to boost the Sox back up on top. For the rest of the season, he didn't blow a save, though he lost four games. (At the start of the 1989 season, he saved 11 more games. On June 5, he blew another save.)

For a left-handed reliever, the number of consecutive saves is considerably smaller: 24 (Tom Burgmeier, 1980). Burgmeier appeared in 62 games that year, finishing 38 of them. His record was 5-4 with an ERA of 2.00 right on the nose. In five years with the Red Sox, he was 21-12 (2.72) with 40 saves. His 1980 season was the only time he reached double digits in saves.

The record for consecutive saves to start off a season is 20 (Jonathan Papelbon, 2006). It was Papelbon's first full season with the Red Sox. He saved 35 games that season. In 2007, he saved 37 games during the regular season and ended up a very satisfying year by saving Games Two, Three, and Four of the World Series against the Colorado Rockies.

Papelbon also holds a record by saving 30 or more games for six seasons in a row: 2006 through 2011. As a free agent, he signed with the Phillies beginning in 2012. He is, by far, the team leader in saves, with 219. The next closest are Bob Stanley (132) and Craig Kimbrel (108). Dick Radatz closely follows Kimbrel, with 104.

GIVEN A CHANCE TO START A GAME, THESE FORMER RELIEVERS SHUT OUT THE OPPOSITION IN THEIR FIRST START

We'll end with a quirky little thing. There are three Red Sox pitchers who had previously worked in relief but, when given their first major-league start, shut out the opposition.

1. Ben Flowers (August 5, 1953)

Right-hander Bennett Flowers debuted with the Red Sox on September 29, 1951, against the Yankees at Fenway. He got a couple of outs, walked Mickey Mantle, but picked him off to end the first of two innings in which he pitched. In 1953, he reappeared with the Red Sox. As I wrote in Flowers's SABR biography: "After 22 appearances in relief, he got his first major-league start on August 5. He shut out the Browns, 5–0, at Fenway on eight hits. The Sox made three errors, but made up for them with five double plays. Leading up to his start, Flowers set a major-league record at the time by appearing in eight consecutive games from July 25 through August 1. Two of them involved four-inning stints, but the record-breaking eighth game (against the Tigers on August 1) was the briefest outing of them all. He threw one pitch."[10] The one pitch was a wild pitch—a very wild pitch—and he was yanked from the game. Manager Lou Boudreau gave him a start, though, and he came through big-time. Five days later, he lost his second start, 2–0. He got four more starts after that and finished the season with a record of 1-4. In his final five starts, the Sox scored a total of only ten runs for him.

2. Russ Kemmerer (July 18, 1954 [game one of doubleheader])
John F. Green tells the story: "Russ Kemmerer pitched a one-hit shutout in his first major-league start, on July 18, 1954, at Fenway Park, leading the Boston Red Sox to a 4–0 win over the Baltimore Orioles. Deprived of a no-hitter in the seventh inning when Sam Mele's fly ball to left field eluded the outstretched glove of Ted Williams, the twenty-two-year-old rookie recalled how elated he was when Williams approached him in the locker room after the game and said, 'Great job, kid, a hell of a great job.'"[11] Kemmerer, a righty, had relieved in five prior appearances, working 10⅔ innings and giving up 5 earned runs. Still, the Sox needed a starter in the doubleheader, and he got the nod. He did walk five, but as far as hits go, he could hardly have pitched better. And he himself scored the winning run. He walked to lead off the bottom of the third. With two outs, a Ted Williams single and a walk followed. Then Jackie Jensen doubled, scoring Kemmerer and Williams. In three seasons with the Red Sox, Kemmerer started 11 games and relieved in 16; he was 6-4 (4.47). He pitched for three other clubs in a nine-year career, mixing starts (109) and relief stints (193), winding up 43-59 (4.46).

3. Jim Wright (May 6, 1978 [game two of doubleheader])
Jim Wright was also a righty. His only big-league work was with the Red Sox, with a winning record both years he worked (8-4 in 1978 and 1-0 in 1979). His career ERA over his 35 games (17 starts, 18 relief appearances) was 3.82. Wright was drafted by the Red Sox but spent nine years in the minors before making it to Boston in April 1978. He worked in three April games, a total of five innings. His first relief appearance was one hitless inning with two strikeouts. His second saw him walk three in two innings but not give up a hit. The third outing saw him get hammered for six runs (five earned) in two innings. And then he got a start. It was the second game of two at Fenway against the Chicago White Sox. He gave up a lone single in the second and another in the third. Jim Rice hit a two-run homer for the Red Sox in the bottom of the fourth. Wright walked no one. He gave up seven hits in all: five singles, and two doubles to Chet Lemon. Dwight Evans hit a solo home run in the bottom of the seventh. The White Sox never scored, and Wright had a 3–0 shutout in his first major-league start. He got 11 more starts that year and relieved in 5 more games. In June, he threw two more shutouts, a 5–0 two-hitter against the California Angels on June 13 and a 1–0 six-hitter against Kansas City on June 29. In 1979, he won his first outing, a six-inning start on April 25 in which he gave up just one hit. His next 10 appearances were all in relief. A sore shoulder sidelined him for the rest of the season, and he never made it back to the bigs.

V

RED SOX BATTERS

13

BEST SINGLE-GAME PERFORMANCES

As with pitching, there is more than one way to measure performance. When talking offense, the name of the game is runs. Which Red Sox players drove in the most runs in a given game? All it takes is one run to drive in the winning run in a game. Let's say you drove in five runs; there's a good chance you provided the winning run in that game. That's bound to have been a very good game. Let's say you drove in ten runs in a game. You'd join good company. There are four Red Sox players who have driven in ten runs in a game.

Here they are:

1. Rudy York (July 27, 1946)

York played first base for a powerful 1946 Red Sox team. He drove in 119 runs that year, bracketed by Ted Williams (123 RBIs) and Bobby Doerr (116 RBIs.). He drove in more than 8 percent of those runs on just this one day. The team was in St. Louis, and York had driven in 4 the day before. In the top of the first inning, he doubled to right field, driving in Johnny Pesky and Ted Williams. The Browns' Tex Shirley replaced starter Bob Muncrief in the second. His first act was to walk Ted Williams, loading the bases. His second act was to serve up a pitch for York, which York shot out of the park for a grand slam.

In the fourth, York walked. But in the top of the fifth, he came up again with the bases loaded. An intentional walk would have cost Shirley just one run; instead, he served up another, and York again hit it out. He now had 10 RBIs in the game. Perhaps he was spent; he struck out in the seventh and grounded into a double play in the ninth.

2. Norm Zauchin (May 27, 1955)

Like York, Zauchin got in his RBIs early. He entered the game batting .214; he had 5 runs batted in on the season. The big first baseman pounded a two-run homer off Bob Porterfield in the first inning. With the bases loaded in the second inning and Zauchin up again, Washington Senators manager Chuck Dressen called on Dean Stone to relieve Porterfield. Zauchin hit a grand slam. Third time up, in the fourth inning, his RBI double to left field off Ted Abernathy just barely missed going out, but he did drive in Billy Klaus. In the fifth inning, with Abernathy still on the mound, he hit a two-out, three-run homer out of the park. It was still just the fifth inning, but he already had 10 RBIs. Like York, perhaps he had run out of steam. Pedro Ramos struck him out for the final out in the seventh. Zauchin had a two-run homer, a three-run homer, and a four-run homer. With the 10 RBIs, he had tripled his production to that point in the season. Zauchin's only big year was 1955, when he drove in 93 runs—and led both leagues with 105 strikeouts. The most he drove in during any other year was 37 in 1958, when he was with the Senators.

3. Fred Lynn (June 18, 1975)

Fred Lynn was having a very good rookie year. From May 25 through June 15, he had a twenty-game hitting streak. Then he missed one. The morning of June 18, he said he'd only got about three hours sleep and was "feeling real lousy." He decided to come to the park early for extra batting practice. "I hadn't been timing the ball well for a day or so. I have been swinging too hard, had good pitches to hit and messed them up….So when I went into the cage, I just tried to get the rhythm going right."[12] No doubt he was feeling better by the end of the game at Tiger Stadium.

His first time up, he homered, scoring Carl Yastrzemski ahead of him. In the second inning, he came up again, this time with both Rick Burleson and Yaz on base. Another homer off Joe Coleman. His third time up, in the third inning, he tripled off reliever Bob Reynolds, scoring the same two baserunners ahead of him. Three innings to this point with 7 RBIs. Lynn lined out to second to close out the fifth, then singled to lead off the eighth. He had one more shot, in the top of the ninth, and he hit a three-run homer off Tom Walker. It was a 5-for-6 day. His sixteen total bases tied an AL record. It remains the Red Sox record. Lynn was named both the Rookie of the Year and Most Valuable Player in the American League for 1975. In all, he drove in 105 runs, later topped by 122 RBIs in the 1979 season.

4. Nomar Garciaparra (May 10, 1999)

The Red Sox shortstop had been Rookie of the Year in 1997 and placed second in the MVP voting in 1998. On this day early in 1999, Seattle starter Brett Hinchliffe let the first three Red Sox batters reach base. Then Nomar took them all off the bases with a grand slam to right field. Fans arriving late missed it. But they still got to see Nomar hit a grand slam. In the bottom of the third, Hinchliffe let the first man reach base. Nomar homered him home. He fouled out to first base in the fourth and walked in the sixth. But in the eighth inning, he was presented with another bases-loaded situation. This time, the man on the mound was Eric Weaver. This time, Nomar hit one to left field—his second grand slam of the day.

When thinking of Nomar and multi-homer games, we are reminded of his twenty-ninth birthday, on July 23, 2002. The Red Sox played two against the Devil Rays that day. In the first game, Nomar hit a two-run homer off Tanyon Sturtze in the third inning. Later in the very same inning, he hit a two-run homer off reliever Brandon Backe. As it transpired, Backe was still on the mound in the bottom of the fourth, and Garciaparra came up with the bases loaded. He homered a third time. His 8 RBIs helped the Sox win, 22–4.

Nomar Garciaparra in the dugout with Johnny Pesky before a spring training game. *Bill Nowlin photo.*

GAME-WINNERS?

How many of these four 10-RBI games were actually won by the cascade of runs the batter produced? Not surprisingly, three of the four. York's first slam was a game-winner. Zauchin's was not; the game was a 16–0 slaughter. It was Jackie Jensen's sacrifice fly in the first inning that was the game-winner. Lynn's first home run produced the second and third runs in a 15–1 win over Detroit—a game-winner. And so was Nomar's first grand slam.

ANOTHER STUNNING SINGLE-GAME PERFORMANCE

Consider this game: September 2, 1996. The ten-inning game was won by the Red Sox, 9–8, in Seattle. Reliever Heathcliff Slocumb was credited with the win. But there's little doubt about who *actually* won the game for the Red Sox. Mike Greenwell drove in every one of the nine runs. Let's stipulate: that's a pretty good single-game performance.

GRAND SLAMS

For sheer spectacle, though, a grand slam is a very big deal. Hitting two grand slams in the same game? Daniel Nava didn't do it. But four batters did. Two of them we have already encountered: Rudy York in 1946 and Nomar Garciaparra in 1999. The other two are listed here.

1. Jim Tabor (July 4, 1939)
The Red Sox were at Shibe Park to play the Philadelphia Athletics in a Fourth of July doubleheader. The Athletics scored nineteen runs against the Red Sox…but lost both games. The Sox won the games, 17–7 and 18–12. They had thirty-five runs on thirty-five base hits. Jim Tabor had a very big day. In the first game, he drove in the thirteenth Red Sox run with a double in the sixth. If Lou Finney hadn't been thrown out at the plate, Tabor would have had another RBI. Tabor led off the eighth with a homer off Chubby Dean. But it was the second game in which he excelled.

In the top of the third inning, Tabor hit a grand slam off George Caster, giving the Red Sox an 8–3 lead. But the Athletics scored seven runs in the bottom of the third, taking a 10–8 lead. Boston tied the game in the fifth, the score at midgame being 11–11. It might have been a larger lead, but Dean got Tabor to ground out back to himself and then threw Tabor out at first base. Leading off the sixth, Jimmie Foxx walked, and Ted Williams doubled. Lynn Nelson replaced Dean. Joe Cronin walked to load the bases. Lou Finney had his chance, but he hit a fly ball to shallow center. Foxx had to hold at third base. Tabor then hit another grand slam, giving the Sox a 15–11 lead, all the runs they would need. To make things even a little more exciting for any Red Sox fans who may have been taking in the game in Philadelphia, Tabor's sixth-inning slam was an inside-the-park one. It hit off the center-field wall, at 405 feet, then caromed back several yards past Sam Chapman.

Tabor punctuated his day with a third home run into the upper deck in left-center off Nelson in the top of the eighth. In the ninth, Tabor was in the on-deck circle with two men on base when Finney flew out to end the inning.

On the day, Tabor had 4 home runs, 19 total bases, and 11 RBIs.

2. Bill Mueller (July 29, 2003)

The Red Sox were playing the Rangers at The Ballpark in Arlington. After six innings, the Rangers were leading, 4–2. One of those two Red Sox runs came thanks to the solo home run Bill Mueller hit to lead off the third inning. In the top of the seventh, Gabe Kapler drove in one and David Ortiz drove in two. Mueller came up with the bases loaded. On a 2-2 count, batting right-handed, he hit a grand slam into the left-field seats off lefty relief pitcher Aaron Fultz. Rather quickly, it had become 9–4, Red Sox. Garciaparra made it 10–4 with a solo home run in the top of the eighth, and then Bill Mueller came up again with the bases loaded. Now facing right-handed reliever Jay Powell, Mueller batted from the other side of the plate (left-handed)—and hit another grand slam, this one into the right-field seats. He became the first big-league batter to hit a grand slam from both sides of the plate, and he had done so in back-to-back innings.

A few weeks earlier, on July 4, the switch-hitting Mueller had hit a home run batting left-handed against the Yankees and hit another batting right-handed. The switch-hitting Jason Varitek also hit two homers in the game, but both were from the same side of the plate.

3. A Special Case: Daniel Nava (June 12, 2010)

Why mention Daniel Nava? Maybe you had to be there. If you were among the 37,061 fans who flocked to Fenway on June 12, 2010, you saw the first major-league at-bat of Daniel Nava. Nava had never been considered a prospect and was playing independent league baseball when Red Sox scout Jared Porter signed him—for one dollar.

Just an aside: How much did Rusney Castillo get? I believe it was a seven-year, $72.5 million guaranteed contract with the Boston Red Sox, including a $5.4 million signing bonus. But signing Daniel Nava set back the Red Sox just $1.

Before the game, Red Sox radio announcer Joe Castiglione had talked to Nava and recounted something Chuck Tanner had told him. Tanner had hit a home run in his first big-league at-bat back in 1955. "Swing at the first pitch," Castig said Tanner had told him, "because you'll never get it back."[13]

The visiting Phillies took a 2–0 lead in the top of the second inning. Joe Blanton was pitching for the Phils. Sox shortstop J.D. Drew swung at the first pitch he saw in the bottom of the second and homered around the Pesky Pole, halving the Philadelphia lead. The next three batters all singled, loading the bases. That brought up the ninth batter in the lineup, Daniel Nava. Like Drew (and perhaps remembering what Joe Castig had said), Nava swung at the first pitch and homered into the Red Sox bullpen. A grand slam. It catapulted the Sox into a 5–2 lead. (Manny Delcarmen caught it, so Nava was able to have the souvenir to keep.) The final score was 10–2; the grand slam was the game-winner. Very nice. But, again, why mention Daniel Nava? What he did was almost unbelievable itself, but when he came up to bat for the second time in the game, it was in the bottom of the third. There was one out. But guess what? The bases were loaded again. Could he hit another grand slam? Everyone in the park knew it could happen. He got a standing ovation; you can see it on YouTube.[14] Nava took strike one, right down the middle. And on the fourth pitch, he took strike three on a check swing.

Talk about bang for the buck—one buck.

Three Other Slams Worth Remembering

1. July 19, 1948
Facing Fred Sanford of the St. Louis Browns, and batting in the first inning, Bobby Doerr hit a grand slam. The Red Sox won the game, 4–1. That one slam was all that was needed.

2. April 11, 1962
This grand slam occurred not in the first inning, but in the last one. It was just the second game of the season. Bill Monbouquette was pitching against Ron

Before seats were placed above the Green Monster in time for the 2003 season, a home run over the left-field wall often went into the net. Before the game, a worker would climb the ladder and retrieve balls. The ladder is still there on the wall. Look for it. *Bill Nowlin photo*.

Taylor of the Cleveland Indians. Neither pitcher was giving up anything. The score was 0–0 after eleven innings. The Indians failed to score in the top of the twelfth. Monbo was still in there. Carl Yastrzemski tripled to lead off the bottom of the eleventh. His was the only run that would count at that point, so Taylor intentionally walked both Frank Malzone and Russ Nixon. He was hoping Carroll Hardy would make an out or two (or three) without a run scoring. Instead, Hardy homered, earning a 4–0 win for the Sox.

3. June 13, 1968

This was a game that took fifty-two days to complete. It began on June 13. The Red Sox and Angels played to a 1–1 tie, and the game was in the sixth when it was suspended. The Angels had to leave to make their flight back to California. (There were no team charters then.) When play resumed on August 4, it remained 1–1 until the bottom of the ninth. By coincidence, the Angels pitcher had the same last name as the fourth batter due up for the Red Sox. After a single and two walks, Bill Harrelson was removed, replaced by Andy Messersmith. Boston's Ken Harrelson came to bat. He hit a grand slam into the net atop the left-field wall.

14

HITTING HOMERS

Let's talk about home runs for a while. We've looked at some grand slams, but let's look at some of the home run records that Red Sox players have posted. Had things worked out differently and the team kept Babe Ruth (who still holds the team record for grand slams in a single season—four in 1919), we would likely be leading off with the Babe. Instead, there will be more, including Ted Williams, but also David Ortiz, Jimmie Foxx, and a few others. Even Carl Everett.

Most Home Runs All-Time by a Red Sox Batter

1. Ted Williams (521)
Of these, 248 were hit at Fenway Park. And how many of these were game-winners? We didn't calculate this for each of our top 10, but we did for Ted Williams. The answer is 106. Nine of these were in his rookie year, 1939. He matched that figure in 1947 and again in 1956. No one seems to keep track of game-winning home runs, since sometimes they seem almost meaningless. An example is a two-run homer hit in the third inning of a game the Red Sox win by the score of 14–1. But one can research each and every home run and see if indeed it was a game-winner.[15] In all, 13 of his home runs were hit in extra innings; that gives him the team record. In addition, 7 of his home runs were pinch-

hit homers; that gives him the team record. But there was something extraordinary about Joe Cronin and the 1943 season: in that one season, Joe Cronin (the manager from 1935 to 1947 and thus determining who would be asked to pinch-hit) hit 5 pinch-hit homers all in that one season. Ted hit 1 in 1941, 2 in his Korean War–shortened 1953 season, 1 in 1954, and 3 in 1957. He pinch-hit just seven times in 1957, walking twice and homering in three of his five at-bats.

2. David Ortiz (483)

When the Minnesota Twins released David Ortiz on December 12, 2002, Red Sox GM Theo Epstein must have thought he'd been given an early gift for the holidays. Ortiz hit 20 homers and driven in 75 runs for the Twins in 2002. They must have thought they could do better. But his very first season in Boston, Ortiz drove in 101 runs—the first of ten years in which he surpassed 100. The next year (2004) he drove in 139, and then some huge runs in the postseason, including three game-winning hits that same season. He also set the single-season Sox mark, homering 54 times in 2006.

3. Carl Yastrzemski (452)

Yaz was a Red Sox lifer, signing with the team in 1961 and retiring from the Sox in 1983. He inherited left field from Ted Williams, who himself had retired at the end of the 1960 season. In his twenty-three seasons for Boston, Yastrzemski played in 3,308 games, accumulating 13,392 plate appearances. He drove in 1,844 runs. In the process, he homered 452 times. Yaz played in more Red Sox games than anyone else—803 more than number 2 Dwight Evans. He had 11,988 at-bats, which is 3,262 more than Evans. He is number 1 in runs scored (1,816), just 18 more than Ted Williams. He leads the team in base hits (3,419), doubles (646), RBIs (1,844), extra-base hits (1,157), and total bases (5,539).

4. Jim Rice (382)

Jim Ed Rice also spent his entire career with the Red Sox, and when he was ready to play left field, Yaz moved to first base and DH to make room for Rice. Were it not for a broken hand suffered in September 1975, who knows how the '75 season might have wound up? As it was, the Red Sox took the World Series to Game Seven even without Rice. He came in second in Rookie of the Year voting (to teammate Fred Lynn) and third in MVP voting. The 46 homers he hit in 1978 were the most any Red Sox player had hit since Jimmie Foxx's 50 in 1938. An eight-time All-Star, Rice was the league leader in home runs in 1977 (39), 1978, and 1983 (39 again). Twice he led the league in runs batted in.

5. Dwight Evans (379)

Evans led the league in home runs just once, banging out 22 in the strike-shortened year of 1981. But he was steady and consistent and played nineteen years for the Red Sox. There were three years (1982, 1984, and 1987) when he hit 30 or more home runs, and another eight seasons when he hit 20 or more. The totals built. During the decade of the 1980s (from 1980 through 1989), Evans hit 256 homers—more than any other American League player. He also led the league in extra-base hits during the decade.

6. Manny Ramirez (274)

Manny Ramirez began his career with the Cleveland Indians and already had 236 home runs after seven-plus seasons with Cleveland when he signed a large free-agent contract with the Red Sox in December 2000. He was coming off seasons of 45 and 44 homers. He averaged more than 38 homers his first five years with the Red Sox, with a league-leading 43 home runs in 2004. He added 11 home runs in his 43 postseason games for Boston. Ramirez ended his career with 555 home runs; he hit number 500 as a member of the Red Sox.

7. Mo Vaughn (230)

The "Hit Dog" broke in with the Red Sox in 1991, hitting 4 homers in 74 games that year and 13 homers in 113 games in 1992. Then he got going. The year he turned twenty-five, he hit 29 homers in 1993, 26 in 1994 and 39 in 1995. It was in 1995 that he also drove in a league-leading 126 RBIs and was voted MVP of the American League. In 1996, he upped his HR total to 44 with 143 RBIs. He homered 35 times in 1997 and 40 times in 1998. He became a free agent after the 1998 season and signed with the Anaheim Angels. Vaughn added another 98 home runs over four seasons with the Angels and Mets, losing all of the 2001 season to injury. His walk-off grand slam on Opening Day 1998 led to our choice for the most exciting Opening Day in Red Sox history.

8. Bobby Doerr (223)

Second baseman Bobby Doerr was dubbed the "Silent Captain" of the team by Ted Williams, and he is one of the four "Teammates" immortalized by David Halberstam's book of the same title and the statue outside Fenway Park.

He played his full fourteen-year career with the Boston Red Sox (1937–51), never once leading the team in home runs and only thrice hitting almost 20. But he averaged 19 a year, and they added up to 223. Doerr was a nine-team All-Star, and he hit for a .409 batting average in the 1946 World Series, the only one in which the team played during his time with the Red Sox.

9. Jimmie Foxx (222)

"Double X" hit 534 home runs in his major-league career, but he came late to the Red Sox, arriving in 1936 with back-to-back MVP seasons for the Philadelphia Athletics (1932 and 1933) under his belt. He'd been a prodigious home-run hitter for the A's, with 58 home runs in 1932 and 48 the year after that. In 1933, he won the American League Triple Crown, leading the league in homers, average and RBIs. For the A's, he had hit 302 HRs. His first year in Boston paid immediate dividends on Tom Yawkey's investment, with 41 homers and 143 RBIs. In 1938, he led all of baseball with 175 RBIs (still a Red Sox record) and hit 50 home runs, which stood as the Red Sox single-season record until David Ortiz topped it with 54 in 2006. In 1939, his 35 homers led the majors.

10. Rico Petrocelli (210)

Not counting the one game he played in 1963, Rico Petrocelli spent twelve seasons playing for the Red Sox. His homer totals were amassed from averaging 15 a season for his first four years to suddenly exploding for 40 homers in 1969. It was a season when the Red Sox were really out of contention; he just went for it. The American League record for home runs by a shortstop was 39, held by Vern Stephens of the 1949 Red Sox. Rico one-upped him, hitting number 40 on September 29. He drove in 97 runs that year. Petrocelli hit 29 in 1970 and 28 the year after that before dropping off to the low teens.

MOST HOME RUNS IN A SINGLE SEASON

David Ortiz	54 (2006)
Jimmie Foxx	50 (1938)
David Ortiz	47 (2005)
Jim Rice	46 (1978)
Manny Ramirez	45 (2005)

Mo Vaughn	44 (1996)
Carl Yastrzemski	44 (1967)
Tony Armas	43 (1984)
J.D. Martinez	43 (2018)
Manny Ramirez	43 (2004)
Ted Williams	43 (1949)

HANDEDNESS

Foxx holds the single-season record for the most Red Sox home runs hit by a right-handed batter. Davis Ortiz holds the record for a left-handed batter.

Carl Everett? He holds the record for the most Red Sox home runs by a switch-hitter. He hit 34 homers in the year 2000.

HOME OR AWAY?

The title for the most home runs hit in a season at Fenway belongs to Jimmie Foxx, with 35 in 1938. David Ortiz's 32 home runs are the most for a Red Sox player on the road in one year, in 2006. This mark is tied for the major-league record. And that total is the most home runs any ballplayer has hit on the road in a given season.

Jimmie Foxx in Fenway Park dugout, 1940. *Leslie Jones photograph, Boston Public Library.*

Most Home Runs Hit in a Single Month

Both Big Papi and Jackie Jensen tied for the best homer-hitting months in Red Sox history; though more than fifty years separated their accomplishments, they both homered 14 times in just one month. Ortiz did it in July 2006. Jensen accomplished the feat in June 1958.

Most Home Runs Hit in a Single Inning

The answer is 2. No major leaguer has ever hit more than 2, so every one of these four Red Sox players shares the major-league record:

David Ortiz	August 12, 2008 (first inning)
Nomar Garciaparra	July 23, 2002 (third inning)
Ellis Burks	August 27, 1990 (fourth inning)
Bill Regan	June 16, 1928 (fourth inning)

Readers of this book have no doubt been waiting for a Bill Regan reference. Wait, who? Regan played second base for the Red Sox for five seasons, from 1926 through 1930. He hit a total of 17 home runs during that half decade, never more than the 7 that he slugged in 1928. His 75 RBIs that year were also a career high.[16]

More Home Runs Than Strikeouts in a Given Season

There were four years in which Ted Williams hit more homers than the number of times he struck out.

Year	HRs	Ks
1941	37	27
1950	28	21
1953	13	10 (after returning from the Korean War in midseason)
1955	28	24

All in all, Williams struck out 709 times and homered 521 times, a pretty good ratio. With 7,706 at-bats, he struck out only 9.2 percent of the time.

The Red Sox player with the best ratio of strikeout to at-bats (with a minimum of 350 at-bats) is Jack Tobin. In 583 at-bats, he struck out 12 times—2.06 percent of the time. Les Nunamaker was 2.25 percent (8 Ks in 356 AB), and Stuffy McInnis was 2.44 percent (49 Ks in 2,006 at-bats).

PINCH-HIT HOMERS

A little more on pinch-hit homers? Ted Williams hit 7 pinch-hit home runs over the course of his career. Joe Cronin hit 5 (all in 1943), including 2 on the same day, 1 in each game of the June 17 doubleheader. Del Wilber had 4.

Vic Wertz had two pinch-hit grand slams: August 14, 1959, against the Yankees, and August 25, 1960, against the Indians.

Here are Red Sox pinch-hit homers that won games:

Wes Ferrell. July 21, 1935
Felix Mantilla. May 23, 1964
Russ Nixon. June 26, 1964
Reid Nichols. June 11, 1984
Wes Chamberlain. May 9, 1995

Lefty Grove (*far left*) and Joe Cronin (*fourth from left*). Manager Joe Cronin put himself in as a pinch-hitter and homered five times in 1943. *Leslie Jones photograph, Boston Public Library.*

A Grand Slam by a Pinch-Runner

Here's a twist. On July 13, 1959, the New York Yankees were at Fenway Park. In the bottom of the sixth inning, Ted Williams singled, driving in Jackie Jensen to make it 5–2, Red Sox. He took second on an unsuccessful throw to the plate to get Jensen. Gene Stephens came in as a pinch-runner for Williams. Eight batters later, the Red Sox had scored five runs, and it was time for Stephens to come up to bat. The guy who had entered the game as a pinch-runner that inning hit a grand slam.

Most Home Runs as a Team

The 2003 Red Sox hold the record for the most home runs as a Red Sox team. They hit 238 of them. Manny Ramirez hit 37; David Ortiz hit 31; Nomar Garciaparra and Trot Nixon each hit 28 homers; and Jason Varitek and Kevin Millar each hit 25. In the case of Varitek, the 25 represented a career high; he hit 193 home runs in all for the Red Sox, the only team for which he played. This was the "Cowboy Up" year, and the 25 homers Kevin Millar hit was also his career high. Of the 238 homers, 127 were hit on the road. That's also a Red Sox record. The team record for the most home runs hit at home in a given season is 124, established in 1977.

Most Home Runs in a Given Game

Twice, Red Sox batters have hit 8 home runs in a single game. The two games in question are (unsurprisingly) both wins for Boston.

1. July 4, 1977
Actually, it pretty much took all of those home runs to make this game a win for the Red Sox. The Blue Jays were visiting Boston and held a 2–0 lead through four innings. In the bottom of the fifth, George Scott tied it up with a two-run homer off Toronto starter Jerry Garvin. In the top of the sixth, the Jays made it 4–2. Fred Lynn hit a solo home run in the bottom of the sixth, but that only brought the Sox to within one run. In the top of the seventh, two more Toronto runs scored, and it was 6–3, Jays. In the bottom of the

seventh, Butch Hobson hit a solo homer off reliever Chuck Hartenstein. Bernie Carbo then pinch-hit and homered. Now it was 6–5, Toronto, until the bottom of the eighth. With one out and nobody on, Lynn homered off Hartenstein, Lynn's second of the game, tying the score, 6–6. Jim Rice followed with a home run. Mike Willis replaced Hartenstein and was greeted by Carl Yastrzemski homering. Carlton Fisk grounded back to the pitcher for the second out of the inning, but then George Scott hit his second home run of the game. That's how it ended: 9–6, as Toronto failed to score. Eight home runs accounting for all the Red Sox runs, and every one of them a solo home run except for the first one hit by Scott. The 1977 Red Sox finished in second place, just 2½ games behind the Yankees. The Red Sox hit 213 home runs in 1977.

A note of interest: The 1977 Sox hit 22 home runs against the Yankees at Fenway Park. That's the most they've hit at home against any visiting ballclub.

2. September 4, 2013

The 2013 Red Sox team hit 35 fewer home runs than did the '77 team, but they won the pennant and the World Series. David Ortiz, with 30, led the team. On September 4, the Sox were in first place, as they had been since July 31. The Detroit Tigers were visiting Boston and were trounced, 20–4. The first homer hit was a two-run shot by Sox shortstop Stephen Drew, giving Boston an early 2–0, second-inning lead. Detroit scored three runs in the third, but the Red Sox soon re-tied it when Jacoby Ellsbury hit a solo HR off Tigers pitcher Rick Porcello. Detroit scored a fourth run in the fourth inning, but that was the last one they got. Ortiz homered off Porcello in the bottom of the fourth, tying it, 4–4. In the sixth, the Red Sox loaded the bases and the Tigers brought in reliever Al Albuquerque. Will Middlebrooks came to the plate. Grand slam. A little later in the inning, Daniel Nava hit a two-run homer off Albuquerque. With Jeremy Bonderman pitching in the seventh, Ryan Lavarnway hit a two-run homer. Later in the inning, Ortiz his another two-run homer. And Mike Napoli led off the bottom of the eighth with a solo home run. Fourteen of the Red Sox runs were scored on home runs. They would have won the game even without the other six runs or even if they had hit no home runs at all. The home runs made it a game to remember.

MOST CONSECUTIVE HOME RUNS
IN A SINGLE INNING

This particular record was set on April 22, 2007, a Sunday night game at Fenway Park hosting the New York Yankees. Four days earlier, the Sox had won a game against the Blue Jays and took over first place by a half game. They were never dislodged from first place at any time for the rest of season. That had been the thirteenth game of the season, so they played the next 149 games in first place.

Daisuke Matsuzaka started for the Red Sox; Chase Wright started for the Yankees. New York scored twice in the first inning and added a third run in the second. In the bottom of the third inning, Kevin Youkilis flied out to deep right. David Ortiz flied out to left. With two outs and nobody on, the onslaught began. Manny Ramirez homered to deep left center. J.D. Drew homered to deep right center. Nice. On a 1-1 count, Mike Lowell homered to left. Game tied. Then it was back-to-back-to-back-to-back when Jason Varitek also homered to left. The Sox had a 4–3 edge. Wily Mo Pena could have made it five in a row, but he didn't. He took a cut, but he struck out swinging. The Red Sox won the game, 7–6, but the loss was not Wright's. The loss went to Scott Proctor, who gave up a three-run homer to Mike Lowell in the seventh inning, converting a 5–4 Yankees lead into a 7–5 Red Sox lead.

DAVID ORTIZ: BREAKING FOXX'S RECORD

The first home-run king for the team was Buck Freeman, with 12 home runs in 1901. He broke his own record in 1903, hitting 13 homers. A number of "lean years" followed. Doc Gessler led the 1908 team with a total of just 3 home runs. It wasn't just the Red Sox that were low in power numbers; in 1910, Jake Stahl's 10 homers led the whole American League. In 1912, Tris Speaker hit 10, again leading the league. In 1915, Babe Ruth's 4 home runs led the pennant-winning Red Sox team. In 1916, when the Sox won back-to-back World Championships, three different Red Sox tied for the team lead in homers: Del Gainer, Babe Ruth, and Tillie Walker. They each hit 3.

Freeman's record of 13 stood until 1919, when Babe Ruth suddenly obliterated it, hitting 29 homers. Owner Harry Frazee quickly sold Ruth to the Yankees. Harry Hooper's 7 homers led the team in 1920. Del Pratt's 5 led the 1921 Red Sox. This kind of drought persisted through the 1920s; in 1929, Jack Rothrock hit 6 home runs. That led the Sox.

The next time a Red Sox player even reached 20 was in 1936. Jimmie Foxx, acquired from the Athletics, hit 41 that year. And in 1938, the "Beast" (Foxx) hit 50.

Foxx's team record stood until 2006, when David Ortiz matched and surpassed it. He hit number 49 against the Yankees on September 17 then tied Foxx's mark with number 50 on the evening of September 20, hitting it off Minnesota's Boof Bonser in the sixth inning of a home game at Fenway Park. It was the 152nd game of the 2006 season. There were 10 games left on the schedule; Big Papi would have ten more opportunities to break Foxx's sixty-eight-year-old record.

He didn't wait long. The very next day, September 21, the Twins were still in town. Their starter was Johan Santana, who had won the Cy Young Award in 2004 and won a second Cy a few weeks later in this 2006 season. Ortiz was the third batter in the bottom of the first inning. He swung at the first pitch he saw and homered, hitting a waist-high fastball over the Red Sox bullpen in right field. Number 51! The ball was caught by twenty-nine-year-old Joel McGrath of Waltham, who presented it to Ortiz after the game.

David Ortiz—"Big Papi"—takes a swing. *Bill Nowlin photo.*

Ortiz walked in the second inning, singled in the fourth inning and came up again to bat in the seventh. Matt Guerrier was working in relief for Minnesota. He kept throwing the ball over the plate, Ortiz fouling off pitch after pitch. Finally, on Guerrier's ninth offering (with the count 2-2), Ortiz homered again. Number 52!

Ortiz hit two more homers in 2006, to total 54.

Leading the Team in Multi-Homer Games

As it happens, David Ortiz leads all Red Sox batters in career multi–home run games. He had 49 of them.

Times have changed, for sure. As we have just seen, there were two years in which the Red Sox won a World Series, and it hadn't taken that many homers to lead the team. The Red Sox won the World Series in 1915. That team won 101 games and needed only 5 games to beat the Philadelphia Phillies in the World Series. It was a dominant team. The most home runs any position player on the team hit was 2. Not 2 in one game, but 2 over the course of the 154-game season. Duffy Lewis, Dick Hoblitzell, and Harry Hooper each hit a pair. The Red Sox home run leader that year was actually a pitcher. He hit 4. His name was Babe Ruth.

It's worth noting that Hooper had a multi-homer game in 1915, but it was in the postseason. He hit 2 homers in the deciding Game Five of the World Series, including the solo home run in the ninth inning of the game, the hit that gave the Red Sox the run that clinched the Series. It's also worthy of note that Babe Ruth barely played in that year's World Series. He pinch-hit in the ninth inning of Game One and grounded out unassisted to first base. He was never used again—in any capacity—during the Series.

In 1916, no one at all—pitchers or otherwise—hit as many as 4 home runs. And yet the Red Sox again won the pennant and World Series. There were three players who each hit 3 home runs: first baseman Del Gainer, outfielder Tillie Walker, and pitcher Babe Ruth. Ruth, pitching, did win 23 games that year—and he won once in the World Series. As in the year before, it took the Red Sox just five games to win the Series, this time beating Brooklyn. Ruth pitched Game Two, all fourteen innings of it, and won, 2–1. In the game, he was 0-for-5 at the plate with two strikeouts. But he drove in a run, on a groundout, that carried the Red Sox through the first thirteen innings before

Del Gainer knocked in the second, winning run. The fourteen-inning game took two hours and thirty-two minutes to complete.

Now, a moment of appreciation for Tillie Walker: The entire Red Sox team hit a total of 14 home runs. And 13 of the 14 were hit on the road. In all of 1916, only one home run was hit at Fenway Park, on June 20 by Tillie Walker. It was a solo home run in a game lost to the Yankees, 4–1. It wasn't a cheap home run, or a fluky one of some kind. It went over the left-field wall. The opposition didn't have any more success at Fenway that year. Opposing batters hit a total of one home run, too—an inside-the-park homer on July 19 by Bobby Veach of the Tigers. That ball was hit, as it happens, over the head of Walker, playing center field. He had misjudged the ball and came in on it as the ball was sailing over his head. The Red Sox won that one, 4–2.

The first World Series, of course, was in 1903. The Boston Americans played their home games at the Huntington Avenue Grounds. Buck Freeman was the home-run leader on that year's team, with 13. Second on the team was Hobe Ferris, with 9 homers. There was something most unusual about Ferris's 9 home runs: every one of them was an inside-the-park home run (IPHR). One of them, on June 5, was an inside-the-park grand slam. Career-wise, Ferris had 24 IPHRs. Only Tris Speaker had more for the Sox—one more. He had 25. Yes, times have changed. In the twenty-first century, the Sox as a team has just 7 IPHRs—plus the one Rafael Devers hit in Game Four of the 2017 American League Division Series.

JUST A BIT MORE ON INSIDE-THE-PARK HOME RUNS

He was a veteran ballplayer at the time, but after being traded from the Brewers to the Red Sox in 1970, infielder John Kennedy made an impression on his new ballclub on July 5, pinch-hitting and hitting an inside-the-park home run in his first appearance in a game for the Red Sox.

Greg Cadaret was a pitcher for the New York Yankees. On July 7, 1989, Sox left fielder Mike Greenwell hit an inside-the-park home run off him in the bottom of the sixth, producing the fifth Red Sox run in a 6–4 win. A year later, Greenwell faced Cadaret again and hit another IPHR. This one was with the bases loaded—a grand slam. It turned a 5–1 Boston lead into a 9–1 lead; they ultimately won, 15–1.

There had been a couple of earlier IPHR grand slams at Fenway: April 19, 1952, by Don Lenhardt and August 8, 1961, by Gary Geiger.

Ted Williams hit only one IPHR of the 521 homers he hit. But it counted big time. All the Red Sox needed was one more win to clinch the 1946 pennant. The team was 96-40. But then they lost six games in a row. Finally, in the top of the first inning in a game at Cleveland, Williams hit an inside-the-park solo home run off Red Embree. The Sox won the game, 1–0, and clinched the pennant. It was just one of two hits the Red Sox had in the game.

Anyone who has seen video of Bill Buckner struggling to run due to very bad knees might be surprised to learn that the last of the 174 home runs he hit in twenty-two years in baseball was the one he hit at age forty-one, in Boston, on April 25, 1990. It was an inside-the-park home run.

15

DOUBLES AND TRIPLES
AND OTHER FORMS OF OFFENSE

Home runs and RBIs aren't everything. But what else is there? Well, there are other ways to get on base and other ways to score. For instance, there are singles, doubles, and triples. There are even ways to make an out and drive in a run. The sacrifice fly, for example. We've seen that Carl Yastrzemski's career stats lead the team in most of these categories.

Yaz played in more Red Sox games than anyone else—803 more games than number 2, Dwight Evans. He is number 1 in runs scored (1,816), only eighteen more than Ted Williams, in part because Williams simply got on base so much. Even though Williams played in 1,016 fewer games than Yaz, he drew 2,021 walks to Yaz's 1,845. That helped even up the number of opportunities to score. And, of course, every time Williams hit a home run, he scored. Ted also out-homered Yaz. But Yaz led the team in base hits, doubles, RBIs, extra-base hits, and total bases.

Don't discount the walks—the bases on balls. That's a form of offense, too. In some ways, a walk is even better than a single. Sure, a single can drive in a runner from second, while a walk cannot. A bases-loaded walk, though, drives in a run. A walk with a runner on first puts that runner into scoring position. A single can be just a fluke of sorts, a ball that falls in. A walk—if not intentional, and not one that happens because the pitcher is skittishly working around a feared batter—can leave a pitcher more demoralized. A failure to get the ball over the plate four times can be discouraging if the pitcher is indeed trying to get the batter out. Those 2,021 walks Ted Williams earned put him on base…well, 2,021 times.

He refused to swing at bad pitches. In his rookie season (1939), he was just a kid from California. The umpires hadn't learned to be impressed with his plate discipline. He hadn't yet earned any respect in that regard. But he walked 109 times, setting a major-league rookie record that he still holds. And in the course of his career, he had a 20.75 percent walks mark. That means that, of all the times he came to bat, he took a base on balls more than one of every five. No major-league player has topped Ted's mark. That's one of the reasons he also holds the best on-base percentage (.482) of anyone who played major-league ball. He reached base almost 50 percent of the time he came up to bat.

DOUBLES

Let's turn to doubles and triples. Which Red Sox player hit the most doubles in a single season? One could also phrase the question this way: Which major leaguer hit the most doubles in a single season? The answer is the same person: Earl Webb. In the 1931 season (from a Red Sox perspective, a year pretty much distinguished by nothing else), Webb hit 67 doubles. That's a lot of doubles—11 more than hit by the second Sox player on the list, Nomar Garciaparra, who hit 56 two-baggers in 2002. Dustin Pedroia hit 54 in 2008. Tris Speaker hit 53 in 1912. And David Ortiz hit 52 in 2007. Both Webb and Speaker, of course, did their doubling in the days of the shorter 154-game schedule.

So who was this Earl Webb? We haven't encountered him in the book to this point. He was a right fielder who played just three years for the Red Sox: 1930 (when he hit 30 doubles), 1931 (when he hit the record 67 doubles), and 1932 (when he hit 28). In other words, he hit more doubles in 1931 than the other two Sox seasons bookending his record-setting year. He hit pretty well; his average for the three seasons combined was .321. But his 1931 season was a standout. His 14 homers led the Red Sox (the legendary Urbane Pickering was second with 9), and so did his 103 runs batted in (33 more RBIs than second-best Tom Oliver).

What was the story with all the doubles? Holding a major-league record for what, in the year 2020, will have been eighty-nine years is to hold it for a very long time. It's one of the longest-lasting records in baseball. Webb was given a moniker at the time: the "Earl of Doublin'." He'd begun his career elsewhere but was traded from Cincinnati for "Whispering" Bill

Earl Webb still holds the major-league single-season record for two-base hits. *Leslie Jones photograph, Boston Public Library.*

Barrett. After a pretty successful year in 1930, if he found himself setting goals for 1931, it probably wasn't to break the standing doubles record of 64. After all, he hadn't hit half that many in 1930. The record was indeed 64, set by Indians first baseman George Burns in 1926. By the end of April, he had 5 doubles.

Webb hit 16 more in May, including one remarkable stretch when he hit 6 in two days (one of which was a doubleheader). From May 28 through June 5, however, he doubled only once in nine games. By the end of July, his doubling was being noted in newspaper headlines. But in August, he hit a stretch where, for fourteen games in a row, he didn't double at all. He hit only 6 doubles in the whole month of August. That didn't seem like anything special. They still accumulated, though, and on the morning of September 17 (his thirty-fourth birthday), he was at 63, 1 shy of the record. The Indians were in Boston for a doubleheader. Webb doubled once in the first game and once in the second game, tying and breaking the record. In his nine final games, he doubled just twice more.

TRIPLES

As far as three-baggers go, here is the single-season ranking for Red Sox batters. Tris Speaker hit 22 triples in 1913. Ten years earlier, Buck Freeman had led the team with 20, in the pennant-winning year of 1903. It was one more than he'd hit the year before. There are four players tied with 19 triples apiece: Buck Freeman in 1902, both Freeman and Chick Stahl in 1904, and Larry Gardner in 1914.

Note the years. For more than one hundred years, no one has hit that many triples for any Red Sox team. Had tripling gone out of fashion? Some suggest that Earl Webb padded his doubles record by stopping at second base at times when he could have tripled. (He hit 6 triples in 1930 and 9 in 1932, but only 3 in 1931). But that's perhaps neither here nor there. It's safe to assume no one ever held up to secure a triple when they had a shot at an inside-the-park home run.

Working backward, there are recent seasons, such as 2006, when no one on the team hit more than 2 triples. The most recent time any Sox player banged out more than a dozen was 2003, when Nomar Garciaparra hit a baker's dozen (13). In 1978, Jim Rice hit 15.

SACRIFICE FLIES

The king of sacrifice flies for the Red Sox is either Jackie Jensen or Carl Yastrzemski. It depends on whether you're talking a single season or a career. It's no surprise, perhaps, that Yaz holds the team record for most sacrifice flies in a career. He had 105 of them. But given how many years he played, that's really only 4.6 per year.

Sac flies were apparently not a big feature of the Red Sox attack. Among the single-season leaders, the top thirty-nine American League batters are all non–Red Sox players. The most that any player had in a season was 17 (Bobby Bonilla and Roy White). For the Red Sox, though, the highest number any player hit in a year was Jackie Jensen (12). He did this twice, once in 1955 and again in 1959.

Jimmy Piersall hit 12 in 1956. Five Red Sox players are tied with 11 apiece: Bill Buckner (1985), Nomar Garciaparra (2002), Jackie Jensen (1954), Carl Yastrzemski (1974 and again in 1979), and Kevin Youkilis (2006).

STOLEN BASES

Stealing a base is clearly a form of offense. A successful steal gets a baserunner ninety feet closer to scoring. A steal of home, of course, gets you a run right then and there. Sometimes, a steal of home can be on a double steal. Sometimes—much more rarely—there is a straight steal of home. The last time a Red Sox runner did that was on April 26, 2009 (Jacoby Ellsbury against the Yankees). Before that, the last straight steal of home had been by Billy Hatcher on April 22, 1994.

Twice in 1999, the Sox stole home as part of a double steal: June 4 (Jeff Frye) and August 30 (José Offerman). But, improbable as it might seem, look at June 22, 2014. Red Sox first baseman Mike Napoli stole home in Oakland. Even more improbable? Babe Ruth did it on August 24, 1918. He was the starting pitcher and threw a 3–2 complete game against St. Louis. His third-inning steal of home produced the third, and winning, run.

Jacoby Ellsbury holds the Red Sox record for most steals in a season: 70, in 2009. He obliterated the previous record of 54 steals, by Tommy Harper in 1973. Ellsbury had approached Harper's mark just the year before, stealing 50 bases in 2008. That tied him with Tris Speaker (52, in 1912), the record Harper had broken. Ellsbury stole 52 in 2013. All told, he stole 241 bases in his Red Sox years.

Taking a lead off first base. *Bill Nowlin photo.*

In 2002 and 2003, Johnny Damon stole 31 and 30 bases, respectively. It was the first time a Sox player had back-to-back 30-theft seasons since Tris Speaker had in 1912 and 1913 (and 1914, too). Speaker's were all 40-theft seasons: 52, 46, and 42.

In terms of percentage success rate, Mookie Betts had the second-best season of a player with a substantial number of steals. In 2017, he successfully stole 26 bases in 29 attempts, which rounds up to 90 percent (from 89.655). For his career through 2019, he had an 83.4 percent success rate (126 steals, 25 caught stealing).

Ellsbury, in his seven years with the Sox, edged out Betts for top ranking with a success rate of 83.97 (241 steals, 46 caught stealing). Ellsbury's best season was his last one with the Red Sox, 2013. His success rate was almost 93 percent (.92857), with 52 thefts and just 4 times getting caught.

16

BEST YEARS FOR TEAM OFFENSE

The number of runs scored is probably as good a measure as any of team offense. That is, after all, the main goal of the offense: to score runs. It's up to the defense to do its best to limit the number of runs scored.

Here are the top 5 Red Sox teams for the number of runs scored.

1. 1950 Red Sox (1,027)

The 1950 team scored, as we can see, 66 more runs than any other Red Sox team, and they might have scored even more but for a serious injury that Ted Williams suffered while making a great catch in the All-Star Game. Ted was off to his best start ever, with 25 home runs and 83 RBIs in the 77 games the team had played before the All-Star Break. He was on pace for a total of 166 RBIs in a full 154-game season. After he slammed into the wall, Williams had more or less a dozen bone fragments surgically removed from his elbow and couldn't return until early September. Leading the 1950 team in RBIs were two players, both tied at 144: Vern Stephens and rookie Walt Dropo. Bobby Doerr drove in 120. Even with all that scoring, the Red Sox never got above third place from May 27 on. As to how the broken elbow affected Williams, years later, he told Ed Linn: "I never had quite the extension on an outside pitch that I had before. And I lost a little power." Take him at his word, but looking at his stats in the years that followed, you'd hardly know it.

2. 2003 Red Sox (961)

This team almost got to the World Series, taking it all the way to extra innings in Game Seven of the ALCS. They scored 961 runs, 152 more than they allowed. Three players each drove in more than 100 runs: Nomar Garciaparra (105), Manny Ramirez (104), and David Ortiz (101). But it was a well-balanced offense overall, witness the RBI totals of several other players: Kevin Millar (96), Trot Nixon (87), and three tied at 85 RBIs apiece, Bill Mueller, Jason Varitek, and Todd Walker. Every game of the ALCS against the Yankees was very close; through the ninth inning of Game Seven, both teams had scored 29 runs. It was the 30th run the Yankees scored in the eleventh inning that made all the difference.

3. 2004 Red Sox (949)

The very next year, the Sox took it all the way. They won it all. They allowed 768 runs, a differential of 181 runs. Even though Game Three of the ALDS went to the tenth inning, overall, the Red Sox outscored the Angels, 25–12, and swept the best-of-three series. They faced off against the Yankees again in the ALCS, something of a rerun of 2003. It ended differently, though. As it happens, the Yankees outscored the Red Sox, 45 runs to 41—even with Boston outscoring New York 10–3 in Game Seven. There was that 19–8 Game Three, the game that looked to have nearly put the Red Sox away. Until….

In the World Series, the Sox swept the Cardinals, extracting a little payback for 1946 and 1967, doubling them in scoring, 24–12.

4. 1996 Red Sox (928)

The 1996 team scored 928 runs but allowed an almost-equal 921. Despite ranking so high in runs scored, the team finished third, in the middle of the pack in the American League East. The Yankees, scoring 1 run below the league average, went on to win both the pennant and the World Series. Mo Vaughn's 143 runs batted in led the team by a huge margin; second and third were José Canseco (82) and Troy O'Leary (81), respectively. The Red Sox team ERA was 4.98. Starting pitchers Tim Wakefield and Tom Gordon allowed 151 runs (121 earned) and 143 runs (134 earned), respectively.

5. 2005 Red Sox (910)

The two big boppers accounted for nearly 300 runs each. David Ortiz drove in 148 runs, and Manny Ramirez drove in 144. A distant third was Johnny Damon, with 75 RBIs. This team allowed 805 runs. They qualified for the postseason but were quickly swept by the ultimate World Champion Chicago White Sox, who outscored them 24–9 in the ALDS.

THE ONLY TWO OTHER Sox teams to score more than 900 runs in a season were the 1948 Red Sox (907 runs scored) and the 1938 Red Sox (902 runs scored.)

RUN DIFFERENTIAL

A quick measure of both offense and defense together is expressed in run differential: how many more runs did a team score than it allowed?

The top 10 Red Sox teams in terms of run differential are as follows:

Team	Runs Scored	Runs Allowed	Differential
1912 Red Sox	799	544	255
1949 Red Sox	896	667	229 (154-game season)
2018 Red Sox	876	647	229 (162-game season)
1950 Red Sox	1,027	804	223
2007 Red Sox	867	657	210
1903 Americans	708	504	204
1946 Red Sox	792	594	198
2013 Red Sox	853	656	197
2002 Red Sox	859	665	194
1948 Red Sox	907	720	187

Curiosity leads to the question: What Red Sox teams performed most poorly in run differential? Unfortunately, we've come across these teams already. The ones with more than a 200-run differential were the following:

Team	Runs Scored	Runs Allowed	Differential
1932 Red Sox	566	915	-349
1925 Red Sox	639	922	-283
1926 Red Sox	562	835	-273
1923 Red Sox	584	809	-225
1906 Americans	463	706	-225
1930 Red Sox	612	814	-202

As we quickly see, the 1906 team scoring only 463 runs makes it by far the worst-scoring team in franchise history. The 1907 scored only 3 more (progress!), but they allowed 558, not 706, a run differential of only 92 runs, far better than the 349 differential of the year before.

The 1918 team was third lowest in terms of runs scored (474). But they allowed even fewer…and won the pennant and World Series. They won the pennant in part because they allowed only 380 runs. One big reason for the low totals in both runs scored and runs allowed was that the season ran just 126 games, shortened because of World War I.

VI

COMEBACKS, BLOWOUTS, AND OTHER GREAT GAMES

17

COMEBACKS

OK, so June 18, 1961, was the biggest comeback game in team history. What were some others? Of course, the greatest comeback of all was in the 2004 ALCS, down three games to none, facing elimination and winning the final four games. But we're talking comeback games. The ranking of these games is by win probability; the calculations were done by Tom Ruane at Retrosheet.

Here are the top 10 comeback games for the Red Sox:

1. June 18, 1961
The biggest comeback in Red Sox history happened on this day in 1961 at Fenway Park. The Senators led, 7–5, after six innings. The score was the same after eight, but the Sox were still in it. When Billy Muffett allowed a single and a double in the top of the ninth, Sox manager Pinky Higgins decided to bring in Ted Wills to get the two outs needed to get out of the inning and give Boston a fighting chance in the bottom of the ninth. Wills gave up a single and one run scored. Then he walked a batter. The next Washington batter, Willie Tasby, hit a grand slam. Oops. Suddenly, the Senators had five more runs and a 12–5 lead. There was a second game planned for the day's doubleheader, but one could imagine that quite a few people left the park. But it wasn't over. See the detail of the inning in chapter 19 below. Suffice it to say, for purposes here, the Red Sox had two outs and Don Buddin on first base—but then they scored seven runs to tie the game (four runs coming on a grand slam of their own, by Jim Pagliaroni). Not stopping there, not

content with sending it to extra innings, they drew a base on balls, Buddin singled for the second time in the inning, and then Russ Nixon singled in the runner from second base. The Sox had scored eight runs to come from far, far behind and win the game, 13–12. (They won the second game, too, on a Pagliaroni homer, in the bottom of the thirteenth.) For those who stuck around, it was quite a day.

2. May 13, 1911
The Sox were playing the Detroit Tigers at the latter's Bennett Park this Saturday afternoon. Ed Willett started for the Tigers, and Ed Karger started for the Red Sox. After three innings, Karger was gone, having surrendered 6 runs (4 of them on a Ty Cobb grand slam). Charley Hall worked the next two innings and gave up 4 more runs. It was 10–1, Tigers, after five innings. Some sitting at home might have switched off their TV sets, except that television had not yet been invented. The only people to see (or hear) the game were the people in the stands, most of whom were likely delighted Detroit fans. Boston batters put 2 runs across in the top of the sixth and another in the seventh. It was still 10–4. In the top of the ninth, Harry Hooper was up first, but he grounded out to second base. Then Larry Gardner singled to deep short and Tris Speaker got an infield hit himself. Duffy Lewis doubled, Clyde Engle singled, and so did Heinie Wagner. Willett was replaced by reliever Ralph Works, but Rip Williams swung at the first pitch and singled. Bill Carrigan popped up to short for the second out. Joe Riggert, pinch-hitting for the pitcher, Jack Killilay, tripled to right field. The *Boston Globe* reported "great uneasiness in the grandstands."[17] The Red Sox had scored 6 runs and tied the game. Hooper then grounded again to second, but this time an error was committed, and Riggert scored the go-ahead run. The Sox were up by 1 run. The Tigers scored once in the bottom of the ninth, but Boston put 2 runs across in the top of the tenth. Speaker singled, spraining his ankle colliding with the Tigers first baseman. He had to be carried off the field. A pinch-runner was sacrificed to second. Wagner singled, driving in the pinch-runner, and then Williams doubled to left, scoring Wagner. The Sox held the lead, winning 13–11.

3. June 8, 1937
The Red Sox were in fifth place, with an 18-18 record, and they were in Cleveland. The Indians had first place in sight. Left-hander Archie McKain started for Boston, and he gave up 1 run in each of the first three innings. Boston got one in the top of the fourth and, with a runner on second, hoped

for another, pinch-hitting for McKain. The gambit didn't work. They did score once more in the sixth, but the Indians came back with 4 more runs (on two hits, a hit-by-pitch, and two errors). After eight innings, it was 8–2, Indians. Cleveland starter Johnny Allen was still in the game. In the top of the ninth, he walked pinch-hitter (and rookie) Bobby Doerr. Buster Mills singled, and Doerr went to second base. Mel Almada singled, a Texas leaguer to left, scoring Doerr. Joe Cronin singled, scoring Mills. Still no one was out, so Indians manager Steve O'Neill summoned Joe Heving in relief. Jimmie Foxx doubled to left, scoring both Cronin and Almada. Then Boob McNair doubled, too, but Foxx had to hold up at third. In both cases, Indians left fielder Moose Solters misplayed the ball by being out of position. Third baseman Pinky Higgins singled, driving in Boston's fifth run of the inning. The score was now 8–7, and there was still nobody out. O'Neill made another move, having Heving depart and calling on Whit Wyatt. The first batter Wyatt faced was Fabian Gaffke. He doubled, knocking in both baserunners and giving the Red Sox a 9–8 edge. The Sox had made seven hits in succession. Gene Desautels bunted, grounding out but advancing Gaffke to third. Pitcher Wes Ferrell was asked to pinch-hit for Doerr, and he

Troy O'Leary seen from inside the left-field scoreboard. During the first game the author worked inside the scoreboard (September 21, 2000), the Indians scored seven runs in the top of the first, but O'Leary tied the score with a three-run homer in the bottom of the third. *Bill Nowlin photo.*

hit a sacrifice fly to make it 10–8. Johnny Marcum earned a save for the Red Sox by pitching a 1-2-3 bottom of the ninth.

With a win, the Indians would have attained first place. Instead, wrote Sam Otis in the *Plain Dealer*, "Tossed aside like so many toy balloons in a twister, the tribesmen recovered consciousness to find themselves a full game behind the White Sox and Yankees."[18] Mel Webb of the *Boston Globe* wrote, "It was the rally of rallies for the year, and when it was all over the Boston dressing room was a mad house."[19]

4. August 5, 1938

Lefty Grove was pitching for Boston and Elden Auker for Detroit in a game at Briggs Stadium. Boston scored once in the top of the first, and the Tigers scored three times in the bottom of the second. The Red Sox tied it up with a pair in the fifth, but the Tigers took a 4–3 edge in the bottom of the inning. It looked like the Tigers put the game away, scoring 4 more runs in the bottom of the seventh, even more so when the Red Sox failed to answer in the eighth. In the top of the ninth, the Sox were losing, 8–3. Then the Boston batters got to work. Johnny Peacock did his part by working a base on balls. Leo Nonnenkamp pinch-hit for Joe Heving (the same Heving who had been with the Indians in the 1937 game just cited), and he singled to left field. Doc Cramer singled to short left, but Peacock had to hold at third base. The bases were loaded with nobody out. Red Sox left fielder Joe Vosmik hit a fly ball to center, and Peacock tagged up and scored. Jimmie Foxx hit the ball hard to Billy Rogell at shortshop, and he couldn't handle the ball. The bases were thus re-loaded. Red Sox shortstop (and manager) Joe Cronin was up next, and he hit two hard fouls to left field, then hit one to right field, "spanked… into the right-field seats."[20] A grand slam. And a tie game. Cronin had driven in seven of the eight Red Sox runs.

In the top of the tenth inning, Cramer doubled off the left-field wall. And then Vosmik doubled off the left-field wall. That brought home Cramer, and the Sox had a 9–8 lead. Jim Bagby pitched both the bottom of the ninth and the bottom of the tenth without giving up a hit and booked his ninth win of the season. Mel Webb concluded his piece for the *Globe* in wording reminiscent of the 1937 comeback: "The finish today boosted the morale of the club sky high, and the Sox dressing room when it was all over sounded like the quarters of a winning football team. Surely the boys were entitled to feel happy, for their victory was a full-team affair."

5. April 21, 1946

In 1946, the Red Sox opened the season with four wins in a row. On April 21, they played a Sunday doubleheader against the visiting Philadelphia Athletics. Boo Ferriss, who had won 21 games in 1945, was Boston's starting pitcher. He didn't last all that long. On a pair of home runs, he gave up 3 runs in the first inning. In the third inning, he got a couple of outs but then gave up two walks, four singles and four more runs. With a 7–0 lead, which still held after five innings, it was looking like the short Sox streak was likely over. But the Sox scored five times in the bottom of the sixth. The Athletics didn't wait long; they scored 3 more runs in the top of the seventh. It was 10–5, in Philadelphia's favor, and they tacked on an 11th run in the top of the ninth. In the bottom of the ninth, Boston's Hal Wagner singled and Rip Russell doubled. A walk to Dom DiMaggio loaded the bases. A walk to Johnny Pesky forced in a run. Ted Williams singled, driving in two. Bobby Doerr and Rudy York both made outs, but then Catfish Metkovich hit a three-run homer a dozen rows deep into the right-field seats to tie the game. Two walks but no runs for the A's in the top of the tenth. The Red Sox came up to bat. After one out, pitcher Joe Dobson singled. An error at second base allowed Dom to reach base. And then Pesky walked. Bases loaded. Ted Williams at the plate. He singled to center, and the game was over: Boston 12, Philadelphia 11. The Sox lost the second game, 5–0, in five innings, the game abbreviated because of what the *Globe*'s Gerry Moore called "the silly Sunday curfew."[21]

6. July 3, 1940

The third-place Red Sox were only three games behind the Cleveland Indians. They played a doubleheader against Philadelphia on July 2 and had one scheduled against the Yankees for the Fourth of July. They played a 3:00 p.m. Wednesday afternoon game against the Athletics. The game drew just twenty-four hundred people. And they were likely pretty discouraged when the Athletics built up an 8–0 score through the first four innings. Charlie Wagner had lasted only two and two-third innings; charged with 6 runs, he was replaced by reliever Joe Heving. The Red Sox got on the board in the fifth, when Foxx doubled, Doerr singled and Joe Cronin homered. That made it 8–3. But Philadelphia added two more in the sixth to make it 10–3. Jim Tabor hit a three-run homer in the bottom of the eighth. The Athletics scored once more in the top of the ninth on a solo homer by Sam Chapman. In the bottom of the ninth, Cronin walked. With one out, Dom DiMaggio pinch-hit for Heving and singled. Lou Finney singled and drove in Cronin. Reliever Chubby Dean replaced Athletics starter Herman Besse.

Doc Cramer singled, scoring DiMaggio. Then Ted Williams hit a three-run homer off the back wall of the visitors' bullpen to tie the game. A's manager Connie Mack beckoned in another pitcher, Nels Potter, to face Jimmie Foxx. Foxx homered just inside the left-field foul pole and into the net. Boston scored 6 runs in the bottom of the ninth. Victory.

After taking over in the top of the third, Heving pitched the rest of the game. Even though he gave up 5 runs, he got the win.

7. September 5, 2018

The Red Sox had already won 96 games when this day in Atlanta began. They played the Braves in a 12:10 p.m. early afternoon game at Sun Trust Park. The Braves scored 2 runs in the first off Boston starter Hector Velasquez. He worked four innings, leaving the game for a pinch-hitter in the bottom of the fourth. It was a one-run game at the time. Drew Pomeranz came in to pitch to the Braves in the fifth. Walk, single, single, walk, a run-producing groundout and a triple. Enough. Manager Alex Cora brought in William Cuevas to replace Pomeranz. A single drove in the fifth run of the inning. Then there was a base on balls and two strikeouts. It was 7–1, Atlanta.

The Red Sox went down 1-2-3 in the sixth and 1-2-3 in the seventh. The Sox started the eighth inning with a single, a single, and a single. Bases loaded. Blake Swihart doubled to center-right, driving in 2 runs. A new pitcher came in, and Andrew Benintendi singled, driving in another run. Steve Pearce pinch-hit for Mitch Moreland; he drove the ball to left field, deep enough to drive in a run with a sacrifice fly. The Braves brought in a third pitcher, and the Sox had Ian Kinsler pinch-hit for Rafael Devers. Kinsler singled and drove in 2 more runs. The score was now 7–7, and the large Atlanta lead had been erased. Red Sox reliever Brandon Workman gave up a solo home run in the bottom of the eighth. In the top of the ninth, Braves reliever A.J. Minter gave up a two-run homer to Brandon Phillips. For Phillips, it was his first major-league game for nearly a year (since September 30, 2017). It was 9–8, Boston. That was the score at game's end. Peter Abraham of the *Boston Globe* called it "the most exciting victory in a spectacular season." He couldn't know how the postseason would unfold, with the Red Sox again World Champions for the fourth time in fifteen years.

8. May 30, 1931

On May 27, May 30, and May 31, the Red Sox played doubleheaders, all at home. After being shut out 5–0 in the first game of the May 30 doubleheader, they had lost 11 of their last 12 games. (The 1931 club finished with a 62-90 record.) That first game had been a tight one, Philadelphia's Lefty Grove against Boston's Jack Russell, with neither team scoring through the first eleven innings. The reigning world champion Athletics got to Russell and scored five runs in the top of the twelfth, kicked off by a Mule Haas homer into the right-field bleachers and featuring Grove himself driving in the fifth run. In the second game, the A's scored first, 2 runs coming in on an error in the second inning. A two-run homer by their pitcher, Ray Mahaffey, made it 4–0 in the fourth, and then Jimmie Foxx (with the A's at the time) doubled in a fifth run in the fifth. The score was the same 5–0 by which they had won the first game. And so it stood until the bottom of the ninth. The names of the Red Sox players of 1931 are not widely remembered today, but here is how it unfolded from there. Gene Rye singled. Tom Oliver tripled. The Red Sox were not going to be shut out twice in the same day, by identical scores. Catcher Charlie Berry grounded out, but Oliver scored on the play. (After his catching career, Berry was an American League umpire for twenty-one seasons.) Pinch-hitter Otis Miller singled and then scored when Hal Rhyne doubled. In the tenth inning of the first game, Miller had hit a very deep fly ball to right-center with the bases loaded and two outs.

Connie Mack decided it was a good time to replace Mahaffey and called on Eddie Rommel (after his pitching career, an American League umpire for twenty-two seasons). Rommel walked Jack Rothrock. Bill Sweeney singled, scoring Rhyne. Rube Walberg replaced Rommel on the mound. First, he threw a wild pitch. Then he walked Earl Webb. The Athletics still led, 5-4, but there was just one out and runners on all three bases. Red Sox third baseman Urbane Pickering doubled to left-center, scoring both Rothrock and Sweeney and winning the game in a walk off, 6–5.

The games were held at Braves Field, due to its larger capacity, and about twenty-five thousand fans watched the contests. Burt Whitman of the *Boston Herald* wrote: "It was a game for the book and one that Mack probably never will forget. It should be a good talking point for him whenever his world titles get too cocky and chesty."[22]

9. May 13, 2007

It was still fairly early in the season, but the Red Sox already held a seven-game lead over the closest contenders in the AL East. (The Yankees and Orioles were both tied for second.) The Orioles were at Fenway Park for a sold-out Sunday afternoon game. They jumped on Sox starter Josh Beckett for two runs in the top of the first. They added a run in the fifth, added a run in the seventh, and added another in the top of the eighth. When the Red Sox came up to bat in the bottom of the ninth, they faced a 5–0 deficit. Baltimore starter Jeremy Guthrie was still pitching. J.C. Romero was the fifth pitcher the Red Sox had used. He'd closed out the eighth and pitched the ninth.

Leading off for the Red Sox in the ninth was Julio Lugo. He grounded out to his counterpart at short. Coco Crisp popped up weakly to the catcher but reached first base when the wind-blown ball squirted out of the catcher's glove. Relief pitcher Danys Baez came in to try to shut it down. David Ortiz doubled to deep center, scoring Crisp. At least the Sox weren't going to be shut out. Wily Mo Pena, who had come in to replace Manny Ramirez (tight hamstring) in left field, singled. Chris Ray took over pitching for the O's. He walked J.D. Drew, loading the bases, and then he walked Kevin Youkilis, forcing home a second run. Now the winning run was at home plate. But Sox fans had learned over many years not to get too excited about possibilities that presented themselves. The batter, Jason Varitek, did not hit a game-winning grand slam, but he did double to right-center, driving in two more runs. Now it was 5–4, Orioles, with runners on second and third and still just one out. This was something of a real possibility, to at least tie the game. Eric Hinske was intentionally walked to load the bases and set up a play at any base. Alex Cora hit a high hopper to a drawn-in infield, with Baltimore second baseman Brian Roberts fielding the ball and throwing it to the plate and getting Youkilis. Had instant replay been in effect, the call might well have been overturned. In any event, there were now two outs, Sox still down by a run. Julio Lugo was back up again, and once more he hit an infield roller headed toward O's first baseman (and ex-2004 Sox) Kevin Millar. Ray ran over to cover first base, but he was a little late, and Millar's toss glanced off his glove, allowing both Varitek and Hinske to score, and the Red Sox won it.

10. August 1, 2013

The Red Sox held a tenuous half-game lead in the American League East standings. It was a Thursday night game at Fenway Park. The Sox had finished in last place in 2012, twenty-six games out of first. The Seattle Mariners were visiting. Ryan Dempster started for the Red Sox. The Mariners scored once in the first and once in the third. They scored five more in the fifth inning, four of them on a grand slam by Henry Blanco.

"King Felix" Hernandez started for Seattle. He gave up but 1 run through the seven innings he worked. With a 5–1 lead, Charlie Furbush pitched for the Mariners in the eighth. He gave up a leadoff home run to Shane Victorino, but no more. Heading into the bottom of the ninth, Seattle held a 7–2 lead. Tom Wilhelmsen was asked to close the game out for the M's. After a walk and a single, Brock Holt doubled down the left-field line and drove in a Red Sox run. Jacoby Ellsbury walked, loading the bases. Seattle switched pitchers, summoning Oliver Perez. Victorino singled to right, driving in two runs. Dustin Pedroia singled to left, driving in 1 more. The score was now 7–6, still nobody out, with runners on first and second and David Ortiz coming to the plate. The fans were fully awake again now and primed for another "Big Papi" moment. Nope, he struck out on three pitches. The third Seattle reliever came in from the bullpen, Yoervis Medina. Jonny Gomes stepped into the batter's box. On the seventh pitch, he singled up the middle, and the score was tied. On six pitches, Stephen Drew walked. The bases were loaded, and there was still just one out. The outfielders came in to play shallow, close enough that they could throw the ball to the plate if a fly were hit their way. The infield was poised to throw home or pull off an inning-ending double play to send the game into extra innings. On the first pitch he was thrown, Daniel Nava drove the ball four hundred feet to the warning track in deep center—recorded in the books as a single. In all, six runs were scored in the bottom of the ninth. The game was over. Dempster (charged with all seven Seattle runs) was off the hook; Steven Wright got the win.

"In a word—magical," said Red Sox manager John Farrell after the game. PS: The Red Sox went on to win the 2013 World Series.

18

BLOWOUT GAMES

We've looked at comebacks. What about pure blowouts? These are games in which the other side never really had a chance. This ranking is done by runs differential. We'll present six of them, four from the regular season and two from the postseason. The largest run differential was 25. If you score 25 more runs than your opponent, yes, that can safely be described as a blowout. All but one of them—the 2018 ALCS game at Yankee Stadium—were at Fenway Park.

1. Red Sox 29, St. Louis Browns 4 (June 8, 1950)
The Red Sox had beaten the Browns, 20–4, the day before but went all out on June 8. It was part of a seven-game stretch in which they scored 104 runs, only once failing to reach double digits. Of the twenty-nine games the Sox played in June, fully fourteen of them saw one team or another score at least 10 runs. Three times, the Red Sox scored 20 or more.

On June 8, the first inning was peaceful—neither team scored. In the bottom of the second, the Sox exploded for eight runs, three on a Ted Williams homer and two on a homer by Walt Dropo. The Browns responded with three in the top of the third, but Boston added five more runs; then seven more in the fourth inning. Given the lead, and the game being at Fenway, the Red Sox did all this in eight innings of hitting. They broke a number of major-league records in the game, including most runs scored (since topped by Texas, with 30 in a 2007 game), most RBIs (29), and most

Numbers stacked inside Fenway's left-field scoreboard. As the runs mount during a blowout, the numbers showing on the scoreboard need to be continually replaced. *Bill Nowlin photo.*

total bases (60, 5 more than the previous record). Their 17 extra-base hits and Al Zarilla's 4 doubles in one game both tied records.

Bobby Doerr hit 3 homers and drove in 8 runs. Both Walt Dropo (7 RBIs) and Ted Williams (5 RBIs) homered twice. St. Louis right fielder Dick Kokos had a complaint after the game: "The way they make outfielders chase the ball, you can't catch your breath when it's your turn to bat." He just thought it was downright unfair.

2. Red Sox 24, Washington Senators 4 (September 27, 1940)

With five games left to play in the season, the Red Sox were in fifth place and the Senators in seventh. Each team could still move up one rung on the ladder. Boston let two Washington runs in to start the game, then scored one of their own in the bottom of the first. (As Ted Williams grounded into a double play, a run scored.) They scored five more in the third, first on another Ted Williams ground out, but then on a two-run Jimmie Foxx single and a two-run Joe Cronin homer. In the fourth inning, they scored ten runs—remarkably, without a single extra-base hit. Walk, walk, error, single, single, walk—and the Senators moved on to their third pitcher of the day, Joe Krakauskas. A passed ball allowed another run in. Then a walk, walk, single, and a fly out, for the first out of the inning. Then a second out, at third base unassisted. A single followed, then a walk and a two-run single by Williams. That was it for the fourth. Doerr hit a solo homer in the fifth. Red Sox pitcher Fritz Ostermueller allowed four runs. The Red Sox bumped up their 17–4 lead, adding seven more runs, with several substitute players seeing action. Another run scored on a wild pitch. Another on a sacrifice fly. Tony Lupien tripled to drive in two; it was he who scored on the sac fly. Eleven Red Sox players collected a run batted in during the game. Williams had 4 RBIs, leading the team. Seven Sox each drove in a pair. And three (including Ostermueller) drove in a run.

The Sox won their last five games of the season and ended in a tie for fourth with the White Sox.

3. Red Sox 23, Detroit Tigers 3 (June 18, 1953)
On a visit to Fenway, the Tigers beat the Red Sox, 5–3 on June 16. Then the Sox struck back the next day: 17–1. The only two homers were by Dick Gernert, who led the team with 4 RBIs. Pitcher Willard Nixon went the distance and drove in two runs. But that was just the prelude to the Thursday game, when the Red Sox scored seventeen runs, again—all in one inning! They already had a 5–3 lead heading into the bottom of the seventh. They put up seventeen, and then added a twenty-third run just for good measure in the eighth on a bases-loaded groundout. But after the seventh-inning stretch is when the Red Sox went to work. Some twenty-three batters came to the plate. Here's the sequence: leadoff single by Sammy White, single, two-run single by Tommy Umphlett, strikeout, double, intentional walk, two-run single by Jimmy Piersall, two-run homer by Dick Gernert. Then a single, walk, two-run double by Gene Stephens, walk, single, flyout, single, walk, walk, single, single, single, and single. Another walk loaded the bases, but a fly ball to left ended the inning. RBIs in the inning were distributed thusly: 3 each to Gernert, Umphlett, and Gene Stephens; 2 each to Jimmy Piersall and Ellis Kinder; and 1 apiece to Johnny Lipon, Billy Goodman, and Sammy White. In the whole game, there was just one homer and two doubles. Tigers pitchers walked nine. Oddly enough, Ellis Kinder of the Red Sox was charged with a blown save, since he had allowed the Tigers to score one in the top of the sixth, tying the score, 3–3. Kinder pitched the rest of the game and got the win.

4. Boston 19, Philadelphia Athletics 0 (April 30, 1950 [1])
This was the year the Sox averaged nearly 6.7 runs per game—1,027 runs scored in 154 games. Before this twelfth game of the season, though, they

were 5-6 and had already lost three games in which the opposition scored in double digits. Hosting the Athletics in a Sunday doubleheader, the Sox put across four runs before making an out: Dom DiMaggio walk, Johnny Pesky triple, Ted Williams single, and Vern Stephens homer. Williams hit a three-run homer in the second inning. In the fourth inning, Pesky singled in another run and Williams hit another three-run homer. Bobby Doerr hit a two-run homer, and Dom DiMaggio hit a two-run double. By the end of the inning, the A's had used three more pitchers and the Red Sox had an 18–0 lead. The nineteenth run came on an error in the eighth. Throughout all this, Red Sox righty Joe Dobson held the Athletics to five scattered hits and two walks and shut them out. The second game was not so easy, but the Sox scored once more than Philadelphia and won, 6–5.

5. Boston Red Sox 23, Cleveland Indians 7 (October 10, 1999)

The 16-run differential stands as the largest margin of victory in any postseason game. The American League Division Series against the Indians began with Boston's bats being anemic. They lost Game One in Cleveland, 3–2, the Indians winning in the bottom of the ninth, and they were clubbed down, 11–1, in Game Two. Things were looking grim. Back home at Fenway, though, they began to feast, winning Game Three, 9–3. Then came this game, Game Four. There were two innings in which they didn't score: the sixth and the bottom of the ninth (since at that point, the game was over). But they put the game out of sight early on, with two runs in the first (John Valentin HR), five in the second (Darren Lewis RBI single, Trot Nixon two-RBI double, José Offerman two-run HR), three in the third (Nixon sac fly and another Valentin two-run HR) and five more in the fourth (Valentin doubled in three more runs). They added three more in the fifth, another three in the seventh, and two more in the eighth. Valentin's 7 RBIs led the effort, though Nixon and Offerman each had 5 RBIs and Jason Varitek had 3.

In Game Five, Troy O'Leary hit a grand slam and drove in seven runs, the Red Sox clinching, 12–8. Advancing to the ALCS despite trouncing the Yankees, 13–1, in Game Three (Pedro Martínez pitching against former Sox ace Roger Clemens), that was the only one the Red Sox won.

6. Boston Red Sox 16, New York Yankees 1, at Yankee Stadium (October 8, 2018)

This 15-run margin of victory is one shared by two other postseason games: October 17, 1996 (Braves 15, Cardinals 0) and October 13, 2001 (Indians 17, Mariners 2). But this one was the Red Sox versus the Yankees, and it was in Yankee Stadium. It was Game Three of the 2018 American League Division Series. The Yankees had won Game Two at Fenway. If they took both games at Yankee Stadium, they would be the team advancing to the ALCS. They started Luis Severino (19-8 in the regular season), while Boston started former Yankee Nathan Eovaldi. The Red Sox squeaked out three runs over the first two innings, the first on an infield single and the next two while outs were being recorded. But the Red Sox put the game away with seven runs in the top of the fourth. The sixth and seventh runs on the inning came on Brock Holt's triple; he had singled and scored the first run earlier in the inning. In the top of the eighth, Holt hit a ground-rule double to center and was now a home run short of a cycle. Heading into the ninth, the Red Sox led 14–1, and Holt came up with one on and two outs. The Yankees had conceded the game and put in catcher Austin Romine to pitch the ninth. Holt was going for it, he acknowledged later. He hit the first pitch for a home run—the first player in baseball to hit for the cycle in a postseason game.

19

TWO OF THE MOST ASTONISHING INNINGS
IN RED SOX HISTORY

B oth of these innings saw offensive explosions by the hometown team. The first, in 1961, was statistically the greatest comeback in team history. The second came on June 27, 2003. The two were "bookends" of a sort. In the first instance, this game was included in chapter 17 as the greatest comeback in team history), the Sox scored eight runs in the bottom of the ninth. In the second instance, the Sox scored fourteen runs in the first inning.

1. June 18, 1961

In the first game of a doubleheader against the visiting Washington Senators, Washington scored once in the fourth inning, but Boston matched that with two runs. The Senators immediately put four more over in the fifth. The Sox scored one more. Then both teams scored twice in the sixth. It was 7–5, Senators, after six and stayed that way through the seventh and eighth. Washington went in for the kill in the top of the ninth. Starting pitcher Bob Mathias singled and scored on a single. The bases got loaded, and Willie Tasby hit a grand slam. It was 12–5. The Red Sox didn't throw in the towel, though, and this is when the big inning arrived. Don Buddin singled, but the first and third Boston batters made outs. Not one of the next nine batters did, though. Chuck Schilling singled. Gary Geiger walked. Jackie Jensen walked, loading the bases. Frank Malzone walked, forcing in the second run of the inning. Then Jim Pagliaroni hit a grand slam. Suddenly (and improbably), the game was tied. Vic Wertz walked. Buddin singled again. Pete Runnels pinch-ran for Wertz. And then Russ Nixon singled to right field, driving in pinch-runner Runnels. Red Sox win, 13–12!

The Red Sox won the second game, 6–5. That one took thirteen innings to resolve. Jim Pagliaroni won it with a solo home run in the bottom of the thirteenth.

2. June 27, 2003

The Florida Marlins came to Fenway for an interleague game. This was the same Florida Marlins team that had won the World Series in 2003, beating the New York Yankees in six games. But before this last June game, they came to Boston with a 40-40 record and were in fourth place in the National League East, twelve games behind the first-place Atlanta Braves. They scored first, one run in the top of the first. Carl Pavano took the mound for the Marlins. Boston's Johnny Damon doubled to right field. Then consider what came next. Todd Walker singled to center, Damon scored and the game was tied. Nomar Garciaparra doubled. Manny Ramirez homered. Well, OK, things were looking good. David Ortiz doubled. Kevin Millar singled, driving in Ortiz. At this point, Pavano departed, replaced by reliever Michael Tejera. Did he stop the bleeding? He did not. Trot Nixon singled. Bill Mueller drew a walk. Then Jason Varitek singled, driving in both Millar and Nixon. Up for the second time in the inning, Damon tripled, and two more runs scored. Then Walker singled, driving in Damon. The Red Sox had now scored ten runs—and they still hadn't made an out. OK, time for another pitcher: Allen Levrault. He got Nomar to pop up to the catcher. It was now 10–1, Red Sox, with one out. Ramirez singled. Ortiz walked. Millar made the second out of the inning, but it was a productive one: a sacrifice fly. Nixon walked, loading the bases. Bill Mueller doubled, driving in Manny and Papi. Varitek walked, and now Damon was up for the third time in the inning. He singled, driving in the fourteenth run of the frame, but Mueller was thrown out at the plate for the third out.[23] It was 14–1, Red Sox. Imagine being delayed on your way to

Red Sox center fielder Johnny Damon during the 2004 season. *Bill Nowlin photo.*

the park, turning up at the top of the second. In fact, you still would have seen some scoring. The Marlins scored seven more runs, and the Red Sox scored eleven more. Final: Boston 25, Florida 8.

Note: The Marlins experienced another rough inning at Fenway Park on August 29, 2018. They were leading the Red Sox, 5–3, when in the bottom of the seventh inning, the Red Sox exploded for eleven runs on twelve hits and one intentional walk. None of the hits were home runs.

VII

FIELDING

Scoring runs isn't everything. A team has to prevent them, too. Baseball is, some emphasize, a game of outs. For instance, as seen in this book, the 1996 Red Sox scored 928 runs, good enough to rank fourth all-time in the number of runs scored. But the 1996 Sox also allowed 921 runs. They barely scored more runs than they allowed. That's a big reason why they finished in third place in the AL East, with a record of 85-77.

BEST AND WORST TEAMS

The best fielding Sox team ever was the 2006 squad. The team played 12,972 innings and accepted 6,052 chances, with only 66 errors and a fielding percentage of .98910. The smallest number of errors by any other American League team that year was 84. In 108 of the games, there were no errors at all. The most error-prone player that year was Kevin Youkilis. Of his miscues, 5 were at first base and 3 were at third base.

Errors do happen. To have a stretch of twenty games in a row without a player making an error would not only be remarkable but also set a team record. The standing record is eighteen games, from September 13 to October 1, 2016. In case you were wondering, the season ended the next day, and it was only in the ninth inning that pitcher Drew Pomeranz committed an error, fielding a bunt.

The worst fielding team was the 1901 squad. The team committed 337 errors, and their fielding percentage was .943, but we do need to keep in mind that baseball fields were not manicured as well as they are today, and the gloves that players wore would be laughed at by today's major leaguers. In 1901, Freddy Parent alone (he was the shortstop) committed 63 errors. Fellow middle infielder Hobe Ferris (second baseman) committed 61. Third baseman (and Hall of Famer) Jimmy Collins was charged with 50 errors.

BEST AND WORST PLAYERS IN A GIVEN SEASON

The best fielding percentage a player can record is 1.000. No errors at all. Eleven Red Sox players share that single-season major-league record. Not one of them was a shortstop, second baseman, or third baseman. (None of them was a DH, either, even though designated hitters are by definition error-free when serving in that role. That doesn't mean they can't screw up, when at the plate or when running the bases, but they can't commit a fielding error.) Here are the eleven:

Position	Player	Year	Number of chances
First base	Kevin Youkilis	2007	1,080
Outfielder	Jacoby Ellsbury	2011	394
	Jason Bay	2009	325
	Jacoby Ellsbury	2008	336
	Carl Yastrzemski (Yaz also handled 63 chances at first base this year without an error)	1977	303
	Ken Harrelson (when Hawk played first base, however, he committed 3 errors in 147 chances)	1968	249

POSITION	PLAYER	YEAR	NUMBER OF CHANCES
Catcher	Rick Cerone	1988	499
	Pete Daley	1957	309
Pitcher	Mel Parnell	1949	61
	Derek Lowe	2003	65
	Bill Monbouquette	1963	68
	Jack Russell	1929	84

Who were the best fielders at short, second, and third? They are all relatively recent players.

POSITION	NAME	YEAR	FIELDING PERCENTAGE
Shortstop	Alex Gonzalez	2006	.985, (7 errors in 475 chances)
Second base	Dustin Pedroia	2014	.997 (2 errors in 654 chances)
Third base	Mike Lowell	2006	.987 (6 errors in 463 chances)

Clearly, Kevin Youkilis—whom we just saw in the previous chapter had made more errors than anyone on the team in 2006—had mended his ways. It wasn't just 2007, though. He played almost two full seasons between errors. His last error in 2006 was on July 5. The next time he made an error was on June 7, 2008. That was a streak encompassing 238 games and a league-record 2,002 chances. The ball fielded and thrown to him by Alex Cora just glanced off his glove. "Nothing big," as he put it, quoted in the June 8 *Boston Globe*.

Two other players have longer errorless streaks (in terms of number of games) than Youk's, but they are at positions that are perhaps not as demanding. Jacoby Ellsbury had a 290-game streak, from July 20, 2009, through September 21, 2012. That's more than three years (of course, he

Playing third base in this game, Kevin Youkilis charges a ball. *Bill Nowlin photo.*

didn't play every game in there, but 290 games are still a lot of games). A center fielder isn't presented as many chances, though, as a first baseman. Ellsbury handled 707 chances, compared to Youk's 2,002. And relief pitcher Rich Garces worked for more than five years (257 games), from April 30, 1996, through July 20, 2001, but in his entire Red Sox career, he was presented with only 65 chances.

Alternatively, if one measures the length of a streak by the number of consecutive chances covered without an error, Youkilis is way out there ahead of everyone. He has almost three times as many chances as Ellsbury, but Ellsbury is actually in third place. The second-best streak is held by another very demanding defender, a catcher. Jason Varitek made no errors in 1,053 consecutive chances between July 24, 2009, and September 14, 2011. Number 4 is Dustin Pedroia, with 436 consecutive chances without an error from July 20, 2009, through May 20, 2010. No one else exceeded 232, but here's an odd fact to end with: Rico Petrocelli had the longest streak (232 chances) among all third basemen, and Petrocelli had the longest streak (227 chances) without an error among all Red Sox shortstops.

22

BEST FIELDER AT EACH POSITION, CAREER

R anked by fielding percentage, the following players were number 1 at their position:

Position	Name	Fielding Percentage
Pitcher	Bill Monbouquette	.985 (Joe Dobson was second at .980)
Catcher	Tony Pena	.9942462 (20 errors in 3,476 chances during his four years with the Red Sox)
	Jason Varitek	.9935968 (69 errors in 10,776 chances in his fifteen years with the team, 1997–2011)

The best fielding pitcher on the Red Sox, Bill Monbouquette (*second from left*), with Pumpsie Green, Frank Malzone, and Rico Petrocelli. *Bill Nowlin photo.*

POSITION	NAME	FIELDING PERCENTAGE
First base	Kevin Youkilis	.997 (13 errors in 4,968 chances)
Second base	Dustin Pedroia	.991 (57 errors in 6,635 chances)
Third base	Mike Lowell	.972 (40 errors in 1,427 chances)
Shortstop	Xander Bogaerts	.978 through the 2019 season (73 errors in 3,254 chances)
Outfield	Jacoby Ellsbury	.995
	Mookie Betts	.992
	Darren Lewis	.992
	Johnny Damon	.991
	Jackie Bradley Jr.	.989

*Minimum 200 chances for a pitcher, 400 chances for a position player.

23

TRIPLE PLAYS AND DOUBLE PLAYS

How many times have the Red Sox executed a triple play in the last fifty years? Not many. Seven times. Over the entire history of the franchise, the total is thirty.[24] Here's the list of the ones in the last half century.

1. *August 15, 2017. In the fourth inning, the Cardinals' Yadier Molina grounded to Rafael Devers at third base. He touched the bag and threw to Eduardo Núñez at second, who threw to Mitch Moreland at first base.*
2. *August 16, 2011. Sean Rodriguez (Tampa Bay) grounded to Jed Lowrie at third. He touched the bag and threw to Dustin Pedroia at second, who fired the ball to Adrian Gonzalez at first base.*
3. *July 8, 1984. Seattle's Marc Newfield lined the ball to shortstop John Valentin, who then touched second base and tagged the oncoming runner from first. The unassisted triple play was only one of two in Red Sox history; the other was in 1923, executed by George Burns.*
4. *July 28, 1979. At Texas, Al Oliver popped up to Jack Brohamer at second. With runners at first and third, Brohamer shot the ball to Bob Watson at first base, who then threw across the diamond to Butch Hobson at third base.*
5. *July 23, 1979. At Fenway, just five days earlier, the Angels' Willie Mays Aikens lined to Rick Burleson at short. Burleson touched second base, doubling off the runner departing from second, then threw to Yaz at first base, who doubled (tripled?) up the runner who had left first.*
6. *May 10, 1979. The first of three triple plays in one year again involved the Angels. Joe Rudi popped up to Jerry Remy at second base. He tossed the ball*

to shortstop Burleson, who threw to George Scott at first base. Both times, the runners were unable to get back to the bag and were out.

7. *May 25, 1972. The Orioles' Elrod Hendricks lined to Duane Josephson at first base. He touched the bag at first base, doubling off the baserunner, then threw to shortstop Luis Aparicio, who tagged out the runner who had left second.*

By contrast, the double play is almost routine. Nice if your team is in the field. Not at all nice if your team is the one batting. The most the team has ever pulled off in one year was 204 in 1980. In 1908, they executed only 71.

The most double plays any one Red Sox player was involved in (as a fielder)? Over the course of his career, it was 1,507 by Bobby Doerr. He is first by a very wide margin over the next player, Dustin Pedroia, who has been involved in 937. Both were second basemen. Third on the list is George Scott, at first base. Scott took part in 815. First baseman Mo Vaughn is fourth, with 785. And Jimmie Foxx is third, with 707.

The third baseman with the most double plays is Wade Boggs (299, just 13 more than Frank Malzone). The shortstop with the most is Rick Burleson (698), followed by Joe Cronin's 565. Among catchers, Sammy White's 79 makes him number 1. Number 2 is Jason Varitek, with 72.

For outfielders, Tris Speaker is first with 64. Next is Harry Hooper with 56, followed by Dwight Evans with 40. It may be of interest that Ted Williams and Carl Yastrzemski each had 30. Yaz, though, also played first base, where he had 610 (fifth among first basemen for Boston).

The pitcher involved in fielding the most double plays is Bob Stanley, with 38. Frank Sullivan is second with 30.

24

FIELDING MISCELLANY

The player who recorded the most putouts in a nine-inning game was—no surprise—a first baseman. The "initial sack" was exceptionally busy for Bill Sweeney on June 24, 1931. The game was in Cleveland, and the Red Sox won, so the Boston defense had to record twenty-seven outs. All but six of them were recorded by Sweeney. That's right, 21 putouts. In one of them, he made the final out in a 4-6-3 double play, or he might have had a chance at 22. Wilcy Moore threw a six-hitter for the Red Sox. Not a single out was recorded by any of the three outfielders.

Rich Gedman caught all of Roger Clemens's 20-strikeout game, so he had 20 putouts in that contest, sharing a major-league record with a handful of other catchers. Bill Haselman caught all of Clemens's second 20-K game but got only 19 putouts, because in the second inning, he dropped the ball thrown for the third strike and had to throw to first base, where Mo Vaughn got the putout and Haselman had to settle for an assist.

Aside from first basemen and catchers, it was an outfielder who came in third: center fielder Jacoby Ellsbury, on May 20, 2009. That ties him for the major-league record for putouts in a nine-inning game by any outfielder.

The most assists in a nine-inning game was 11. Four players had 11 each: second baseman Hobe Ferris in a 1905 game and three shortstops (Topper Rigney in a 1928 game, Eddie Bressoud in 1962, and Rick Burleson in 1977).

The most assists by an outfielder? Reggie Smith had three in a game on September 23, 1972. That was pretty impressive, but what about Ira Flagstead? On September 9, 1923, he had three assists in a game against the

Yankees. And on April 19, 1926, playing center field against the Athletics in the second game of a doubleheader, he earned assists in three double plays, each time the second out being a runner tagged out at home plate.

Multiple double plays in a nine-inning game? The Red Sox record is five, a mark shared by many players.

Standing around doing next to nothing? Two fielders come to mind: Steve Yerkes in 1913 and "Baby Doll" Jacobson in 1926. Jacobson played right field. For seven games in a row (June 17–June 25), he took his position in right field for the Red Sox and never once recorded either a putout or an assist. Now, he did throw in a few balls hit his way, which is good. Otherwise, the batters would have no doubt run all the way around the bases. Yerkes was a second baseman, and one can reasonably expect any middle infielder to see a lot more action in a game than a right fielder. But he played all fifteen innings of the June 11, 1913, game and recorded neither a putout nor an assist.

25

HIDDEN-BALL TRICK

You could go to baseball games all your life and never see a hidden-ball tick. Even if you're always on the lookout. (Obviously, the base runner caught off the bag was not on the lookout, but it's such an embarrassing thing that base runners are taught to always keep their eye on the ball and to pay attention to the coaches, who are similarly tasked.) In 119 years, there have been 18 hidden-ball tricks successfully executed by a Red Sox player. The last time it happened was on June 8, 2007. There hadn't been one

Jason Varitek meets with fans visiting from a hospital charity he supported. *Bill Nowlin photo.*

Jimmy Fund collection box. It was the first official Red Sox charity, dating back to the early 1950s. *Bill Nowlin photo*.

for 16 years, since Steve Lyons did it on May 13, 1991. Before that, oddly enough, Marty Barrett pulled it off three times in 3 years, including twice in July 1985, just two weeks apart to the day—against the same California Angels team! Look it up: On July 7, 1985, then July 21, 1985, and, lastly, on September 5, 1988.

VIII

OBSCURITIES AND ODDBALL LISTS

26

MOST OBSCURE RED SOX PLAYERS OF ALL TIME

John Smith? Tony Renda? What constitutes an obscure player? Someone you didn't know played for the team. It might not be someone who played in just one game. It could be someone who played in four games! Particularly if they had bestowed on them a name as bland (if that does not seem unfair) as John Smith. There are other players who have participated in very few games, even in recent years, but sometimes their names are more memorable.

As for John Smith, he was one of the very first members of the Red Sox to be given a uniform number. He played in four games for the 1931 Sox, the first year the team wore uniform numbers. The four games he played were on two back-to-back days; he played first base in both halves of the September 17 and September 18 doubleheaders against Cleveland. He played first base well, handling 46 chances (every one of them a putout) without making an error. At the plate, he walked and came around to score in the first game on the September 17. In the second game, he hit a sacrifice fly that scored Earl Webb for the only run the Red Sox scored. The Sox lost, 2–1, even though Webb doubled in the bottom of the ninth. His double established a new (and still-standing) record for the number of doubles any player hit in a season. It was Webb's 65th (he later added 2 more). Smith grounded out to the first baseman, who threw home to cut down what could have been the tying run.

On September 18, Smith got his first major-league base hit (a single) in the first inning of the first game. In the second game, he got his second hit, another single. But that was it for his career in the big leagues. What number had he worn? Number 9. Next time you are at Fenway Park, you will notice that number 9 was subsequently retired.

Some other names of Red Sox players that might be comparable to Smith's in seeming unremarkable include Bob Adams, Al Baker, Dave Black, Bill Evans, Bill James, and Jack Robinson. (This Jack Robinson did have the middle initial "E." and pitched four innings over three games for the 1949 Red Sox. Just four years before, the Red Sox had declined the opportunity to sign the player more widely known as Jackie Robinson.)

The Sox have also had players with more "unusual" names: Lou Berberet, Clarence Blethen, "Boof" Bonser, Rick Croushore, Elmer Eggert, and "Jigger" Statz come to mind. As one might guess, Boof and Jigger were nicknames but were the names by which they were known. Boof even went to court to make his nickname his legal name.

Some players who might seem obscure played for the Red Sox for more than just one season, and they had memorable names to boot: Asby Asbjornson, catcher (1928–29); Cot Deal, right-handed pitcher (1947–48); Hob Hiller, infielder (1920–21); and Smead Jolley, left fielder (1932–33).

There are other Red Sox players who should perhaps be more widely known than they are. For instance, Dale Alexander. Who was Dale Alexander? He was the American League batting champion in 1932. It was the first batting title ever won by a Red Sox player. He came to the Sox in mid-June 1923, traded on the fifteenth from the Detroit Tigers (along with Roy Johnson) for Earl Webb. This was the same Webb who had just set the major-league record for doubles, with 67 in 1931. Webb wasn't faring well in 1932, however. And Alexander had seen only 16 at-bats for the Tigers. He was hitting .250. When he arrived in Boston, however, Alexander was put to work, playing first base. He started hitting right away. He got into 101 games and hit .372 for Boston (enough to raise his average for the year to .367, winning the AL batting title). Johnson did well, batting .298 and then over .300 for

Speaking of oddballs, Bill Lee cultivated a reputation as same. *Bill Nowlin photo.*

each of the next three years. Webb was out of major-league baseball after the 1933 season.

World Champions are remembered forever. Surely, the last Red Sox team to win a World Championship for eighty-six years would be remembered forever. Some Sox fans were born, lived out their full lives and died before Boston again won a World Series, in 2004. The 1918 team—legends all. Right? Babe Ruth, of course. Harry Hooper, still the only Red Sox player with four World Championship rings. We've encountered him already in this book, too. But what about the rest of them? And we can leave aside players like Eusebio Gonzalez, who appeared just in three games. Or undefeated (1-0) pitcher Vince Molyneaux, who was in six games. Or Red Bluhm, whose one fruitless pinch-hit at-bat is the sum total of his major-league career. There always seem to be a few marginal guys. Looking only at 1918 World Champion Red Sox players who worked in twenty or more games, we have a dozen others.

Sam Agnew
George Cochran
Dick Hoblitzell
Wally Mayer
Stuffy McInnis
Wally Schang
Everett Scott
Dave Shean
Jack Stansbury
Amos Strunk
Fred Thomas
George Whiteman

Immortals, all.

THE YEAR 2014 WASN'T that long ago. Mookie Betts was on that team, and Jackie Bradley Jr. So was Christian Vazquez. Dustin Pedroia. David Ortiz. Xander Bogaerts. Jon Lester. But how many among us really remember Kelly Johnson and Corey Brown? Johnson was actually traded to the Red Sox by the Yankees on July 31 for Stephen Drew and cash. Less than a month later, the Sox traded him to Baltimore for Ivan DeJesus and Jemile Weeks. A utility player, Johnson played in ten games for the Red Sox and struck out ten times. He got four base hits, including a double, and drove

Birdie Tebbetts (*left*), Mel Parnell (*center*), and Vern Stephens. *Leslie Jones photograph, Boston Public Library.*

in one run (with the double driving in Brock Holt). Corey Brown was an outfielder who appeared in three games but had just 1 at-bat, a strikeout. The 2013 team had won the World Series, the last team to win a World Series at Fenway Park since the 1918 team. But the 2014 team finished in last place in the AL East, twenty-five games out of first.

In their first 118 seasons, the Red Sox have fielded 1,795 players. It's not surprising that we can't remember them all. They've had one Bird (Doug) but three Byrds (Jim, Marlon, and Paul). There have been other "fowl" names: Birdie Tebbetts, Joel Finch, Goose Gregson (a coach), Tom Herrin, and Rube Kroh. And some other players have had animal names: Catfish Metkovich, Moose Grimshaw, Jim Tabor, Dizzy Trout, Rabbit Warstler, and Larry Wolfe.

27

MOST OBSCURE WORLD CHAMPION RED SOX OF THE TWENTY-FIRST CENTURY

2004 WORLD CHAMPIONS

The now-classic, legendary 2004 Red Sox team had eight players who appeared in four or fewer games. The position players were as follows:

Name	Position	Games Played	Batting/ Pitching Result
Sandy Martinez	Catcher	3	0-4
Earl Snyder	Third base	1	1-4
Jamie Brown	Pitcher	4	0-0
Bobby Jones	Pitcher	3	0-1
Joe Nelson	Pitcher	3	0-1
Frank Castillo	Pitcher	2	0-0
Phil Seibel	Pitcher	2	0-0
Abe Alvarez	Pitcher	1	0-1

Every one of them was part of the team. So was Brandon Puffer, but you won't find him on Retrosheet or Baseball-Reference.com as a player on the 2004 team. He was, though. Puffer was a right-handed pitcher. The Red Sox purchased his contract from the San Diego Padres on July 2, 2004. On October 14, he was granted free agency. But they had also acquired another pitcher, lefty Jimmy Anderson. So, they put Puffer with Pawtucket. Anderson pitched in five games for a total of six innings. He was released on August

1. When the rosters expanded on September 1, Puffer was brought up to Boston. He spent a total of one day with the team, in the bullpen on the evening of September 2. He was designated for assignment on September 3 so that the Sox could bring up outfielder Adam Hyzdu.

Red Sox ownership, as they have each time, awarded rings to everyone on the team, even if they played in just one game—or none, in the case of Brandon Puffer. He was on the roster, if only for parts of a couple of days. I contacted him in December 2007, and he said, "The Red Sox were extremely gracious including me in the lucky group of people to receive such a special memento to 'The Nation.'" The 2004 team sometimes referred to themselves as the "Idiots." Puffer added, "I think I could have been a great idiot."

Oddly, Puffer did play at Fenway Park in 2004. He was with the Padres at the time, and on the evening of June 10, he relieved Ismael Valdez. He got three outs in the bottom of the fifth, but before he did, he'd allowed two inherited runners to score, and then two more that were charged to him. He then worked two scoreless innings. So, the one game he played that involved the Red Sox was against them. He worked three innings and allowed the Sox two runs.

2007 WORLD CHAMPIONS

There were four players on the 2007 team who appeared in 4 or fewer games.

Name	Position	Games Played	Batting/Pitching Result
Jeff Bailey	First base	3	1-9
David Murphy	Outfield	3	1-2
Clay Buchholz	Pitcher	4	3-1
Devern Hansack	Pitcher	3	0-1

Buchholz, of course, hardly qualifies as obscure. In the second of his games, on September 1, he threw a no-hitter for the Red Sox. Even though he was 2-9 in 2008, he had a couple of very good years for Boston, including a 17-7 season in 2010 and a 12-1 season in 2013. He won 81 games for the Red Sox.

Champagne after the 2004 and 2007 World Championships. *Bill Nowlin photo.*

2013 WORLD CHAMPIONS

There were only three Red Sox players on the 2013 team who worked in four or fewer games, and all three were pitchers.

Player	Games Played	Pitching Result
Steven Wright	4	2–0
Daniel Bard	2	0–0
Brayan Villareal	1	0–0

The Villareal story would be hard to top. He'd been with the Detroit Tigers earlier in the season but came to Boston in time to appear in the August 20 game in San Francisco against the Giants. In the bottom of the ninth, the score was tied, 2–2. Left-hander Franklin Morales got two outs, with a single in between. Then he walked a batter and hit the next. This loaded the bases, but there were the two outs. Manager John Farrell brought in a right-hander, Villareal, to pitch to Marco Scutaro. Without trying to be unkind, what he did is something almost anyone could do. Ball one, ball two, ball three, ball four. Scutaro walked and forced in the game-winning run from third. Scutaro had a walk-off walk. The four pitches were the sum total of Villareal's work for the World Champion Boston Red Sox. He got a ring.

2018 WORLD CHAMPIONS

On a team as recent as the 2018 Red Sox, one might think that none of the players would be a candidate for the most obscure Sox player. Time will tell. There were five who appeared in four or fewer games.

Name	Position	Games Played	Batting/Pitching Result
Dustin Pedroia	Second base	3	1-11
Dan Butler	Catcher	2	1-6, 1 RBI
Tony Renda	Pinch-runner	1	0 plate appearances, 1 run scored
Justin Haley	Pitcher	4	0-0
Jalen Beeks	Pitcher	2	0-1

Dustin Pedroia, of course, is far from obscure. He's one of the most popular players of his time. He was Rookie of the Year in 2007, when the Red Sox won the second of their four World Championships of the first twenty years of the new century. And he was the Most Valuable Player in the American League the very next year. He is a four-time All-Star with a lifetime .299 batting average and three World Series rings. Admittedly, injuries prevented him from contributing on the field in 2018. And he was unable to play at all in 2019.

Justin Haley was granted free agency after the 2018 season.

Jalen Beeks was traded to Tampa Bay near the end of July 2018 for Nathan Eovaldi, another pitcher who became something of a star in the 2018 postseason, winning two games and working twenty-two and one-third innings with an ERA of 1.61.

Tony Renda's one moment was a nice one. Sunday night, August 5 at Fenway. Red Sox versus Yankees. The game was tied, 4–4, in the bottom of the tenth. The first two Red Sox batters were retired. Sandy Leon singled to left. He went to second on a wild pitch. Mookie Betts was intentionally walked. Manager Alex Cora had Renda enter as a pinch-runner. Andrew Benintendi singled to center and Renda scored the winning run. It was the only thing he did for the 2013 Red Sox. Zero plate appearances, zero time on defense. He ran 180 feet and scored the winning run against the Yankees.

28

FIRSTS FROM FOREIGN LANDS

The first foreign-born player who was a member of the team was, as it happens, the starting pitcher in the team's very first game. It was Win Kellum, born in Waterford, Ontario, on April 11, 1876. The first game played by the Boston Americans was in Baltimore on April 26, 1901, attended by ten thousand of "the finest people in this city," according to *Boston Globe* writer Tim Murnane. Winford Ansley Kellum's nickname was, understandably, "Win," but he lost that first game, 10–6. After Boston batters were retired in order in the top of the first, John McGraw led off for the Orioles, doubling to right field. Then Mike Donlin tripled, also to right. Jimmy Williams walked and Bill Keister tripled to right-center. It was 3–0 before the first out was recorded. Kellum escaped further damage in the inning. In the ninth inning, Boston scored three runs, in part thanks to another Canadian, Larry McLean of Fredericton, New Brunswick, who pinch-hit for Kellum and doubled. Kellum was 2-3 on the season, his only season with the team that, in 1908, became the Red Sox.

The first Boston player who did not come from North America was another starting pitcher, the Welshman Ted Lewis. His first game was the sixth game in franchise history, played in Philadelphia against the Athletics on May 2, 1901. He pitched a complete game, too, despite giving up 12 runs. One could well say he benefited from some run support: Boston scored twice in the first inning, nine times in the second, and then ten more times in the third. The *Boston Globe* observed that Lewis "did not pitch gilt-edge ball by any means. It was only good by comparison with the weird work of the local boxmen." Lewis was 1-for-4 at the plate, also drawing a walk and scoring two runs. Despite the 23–12 score, Lewis still got the win. Lewis later became president of the University of New Hampshire.

Players Born in Other Lands

Thus, we have the first Canadian and the first from Wales. Here, we indicate the first franchise player born in each of the countries outside the United States that have provided a player for the team. There are, understandably, many countries not yet represented. Even though they are both parts of the United States, we have listed Puerto Rico and the Virgin Islands as points of interest. We have listed England, Scotland, and Wales separately. This results in twenty-five lands being represented. When a country has had more than one native play for the Red Sox, the number of players through the 2019 season is noted in parentheses after the country's name.

Aruba: Xander Bogaerts

He debuted in 2013. The Xander Bogaerts story is still being told. In his first six seasons with the Red Sox (through 2019), he has two World Series rings, and in early 2019, the Red Sox signed him to a six-year contract extension. As do most Arubans, Bogaerts speaks four languages: Dutch, English, Spanish, and Papiamento. He's a two-time Silver Slugger winner and was an All-Star in 2016. In 2018, he hit 23 homers and had 103 runs batted in. An All-Star again, he set new highs in 2019, with 33 homers and 117 RBIs.

Xander Bogaerts in London, June 2019. *Bill Nowlin photo.*

Austria-Hungary: Jack Quinn

In 1883, right-handed pitcher Jack Quinn was born as Johannes Pajkos in Stefurov, Slovakia, part of Austria-Hungary at the time. He took the name John Picus Quinn. He began his career with the New York Yankees in 1909, the first of two stints with the team. In his seventeen-year career,

Quinn was 247-219 (3.29 ERA) and pitched for seven different teams in three major leagues (AL, NL, and Federal League). In December 1921, he was traded by the Yankees to the Red Sox, and he pitched for the Sox for three and a half years, 1922 into July 1925. For the Red Sox, he won 45 games for teams that never posted a winning record during the years in question.

Canada (24): Win Kellum

In 1901, the left-handed Kellum pitched in the first game in franchise history. He lost each of his first two starts (giving up fourteen runs on May Day) but then threw a four-hitter against Washington on May 7, the last game on the first road trip before the Americans came back to Boston for their first home game, pitched by Cy Young on May 8. Kellum's last start for the team came on June 14, but he was knocked out of the game; Young took over and ultimately won. The team released Kellum (2-3, 6.38 ERA in 45 innings of work). He made his way back to the big leagues and won 15 games for Cincinnati in 1904. Through the 2019 season, Kellum is one of twenty-four native Canadians to have played for the Red Sox franchise.

Colombia (3): Jackie Gutierrez

The first Colombian to play for the Red Sox was shortstop Jackie Gutierrez, from Cartagena. He broke into the big leagues with Boston in 1983. A September call-up, he got into five games and was 3-for-10. In 1984, Gutierrez played in a full 151 games. He hit .263, drove in 29 runs, and scored 55 times. After playing in 103 games in 1985, he was traded to the Orioles. The other two Colombians to play for Boston were both shortstops as well: Orlando Cabrera (who came to Boston at the trading deadline in 2004 and helped the Sox win their first World Series since 1918, driving in 11 postseason runs) and Edgar Renteria in 2005.

Cuba (20): Eusebio Gonzalez

Gonzalez was the first foreign-born Latino to play for the Red Sox. He was on the 1918 team that won the World Series. An infielder, he played in just three games—two in late July and one in early August—but was 2-for-5 with a triple at the plate. The season was to be cut short due to the world war and scheduled to end on September 2. The first-place Red Sox did not truly need another utility infielder and so worked out a deal to place him with Toronto.

The second Cuban on the Red Sox was infielder Mike Herrera (84 games in 1925–26.) One of the more notable Cubans in Red Sox history was pitcher Luis Tiant (1971–78), a player who might well be deemed worthy of the Hall of Fame and who remains a beloved figured in the Boston area.

Denmark: Olaf Henriksen

Not only was Olaf Henriksen the first native Dane to play for the Red Sox, he is also the only one to play for any major-league team. Many may not realize that Henriksen was part of three World Championship teams: 1912, 1915, and 1916. Henriksen was a reserve outfielder for the Red Sox (and no other team) from 1911 to 1917. In the seventh inning of the final game of the 1912 World Series, pinch-hitting against Christy Mathewson, Henriksen doubled to tie the score in a game the Red Sox won in the bottom of the tenth.

Dominican Republic (55): Mario Guerrero

Guerrero was the first of the fifty-five Dominicans who have played for the Red Sox through the 2019 season. Originally signed by the Yankees, he came to Boston as the player to be named later in the 1972 trade for Sparky Lyle. He played shortstop and second base for the Red Sox in 1973 and 93 games in 1974 but was traded to the Cardinals just before the 1975 season. He hit .241 and drove in 34 runs in 159 games.

When Pedro Martinez first established himself in Boston, Fenway Park was replete with manifestations of Dominican pride. *Bill Nowlin photo.*

In 1974, the Red Sox added a future Hall of Fame pitcher: Laguna Verde's Juan Marichal. He was 5-1 that season, his last wins in the big leagues. The list of Dominicans who have played for the Red Sox is an impressive one, both in quantity and quality.

England (3): Albert "Hobe" Ferris

A native of Trowbridge, Wiltshire, England, Ferris played second base in the first game in franchise history. He played 983 games, with a .237 average and 418 RBIs in seven years for the team (1901–07), the seven years before the team became the Red Sox in 1908. He hit .290 with 5 RBIs in the 1903 World Series against Pittsburgh. The other two Englishmen who played for the team were both in the early days, too: Al Shaw (1907) and Walter "Rosy" Carlisle (1908).

Germany (4): Pep Deininger

The southpaw from Wasseralfingen? The community is now part of Aalen, about an hour from Stuttgart. He wasn't with Boston for long. On the same 1902 pitching staff as thirty-two-game winner Cy Young, Deininger appeared in just two games and pitched a total of twelve innings. Six years later, he reappeared in the majors with the 1908 Phillies as an outfielder. The other German-born players on the team were Marty Krug (1912), Tony Welzer (1926), and Tom McCarthy (1985).

Ireland: Jimmy Walsh

For a city that was so heavily settled by Irish immigrants, only one native Irishman has ever played for the Red Sox. Rathroe, County Tipperary, was where Jimmy Walsh was born. He was an outfielder who had played for the Yankees and Philadelphia Athletics, arriving with the Red Sox by way of a September 2, 1916 trade for Raymond Haley. Walsh appeared in fourteen games before the end of the season, batting .176 with 2 RBIs but with a .333 on-base percentage. It was enough, though, to make him part of the World Champion 1916 Red Sox. Walsh had Series experience, appearing in three games for the Athletics in 1914. For the Red Sox, he pinch-hit in the ninth inning of a 1–1 Game Two. He hit the ball right back to the pitcher but reached first base on a fielder's choice throwing error. Staying in the game, he got two more at-bats, popping up foul to first base and foul to third base in the thirteenth. The Red Sox won the game in fourteen.

One other notable Irish native was Red Sox manager Patsy Donovan (1910–11).

Jamaica: Justin Masterson

With a father who worked in the ministry, right-hander Masterson was born in Kingston, Jamaica, in 1985. In 2008, he debuted with the Red Sox (6-5, 3.16). He worked in 36 games, starting 9. In the postseason, he was used in relief in almost every game—4 games in the ALDS and 5 in the ALCS, with a 1-0 record (Game Five of the ALCS), 4 holds and 1 blown save. He was 3-3 in 2009, until July 30, when he was one of three players sent to the Indians for Víctor Martínez.

Another notable Jamaican was major-league hitting coach Chili Davis (2015–17).

Japan (8): Tomo Ohka

It wasn't until 1999 that the Sox had their first Japanese native on the team. Within ten years, they'd have eight. Kyoto—a "sister city" to Boston—was home both to Ohka and 2007 World Champion Hideki Okajima.

Noting world champions, of the eight Japanese players on the team through 2018, five have rings: Dave Roberts (2004), Daisuke Matsuzaka and Hideki Okajima (2007), and Junichi Tazawa and Koji Uehara (2013). Hideo Nomo has a no-hitter to his credit.

Ohka broke into the majors with the Red Sox and pitched parts of three seasons, starting twenty-five games, but he never enjoyed a season in which he won as many games as he lost. He was traded to the Expos in July 2001 for Ugueth Urbina.

Korea (4): Jin Ho Cho

The Sox have had four Korean natives, all of whom were pitchers and all of whom joined the team in what seemed like a flurry between 1998 and 2003. Three were right-handers; the only lefty was Sang-Hoon Lee, and he was the only one without a decision. The only one with a winning record was Byung-Hyun Kim (10-6 in 2003 and 2004); he also faced four batters in the 2003 AL Division Series against Oakland. Jin Ho Cho was a native of Jeonju. He was 2-6, losing his first three of four appearances in July 1998. Having a good season with Pawtucket in 1999, he won the first two June games after he was summoned to Boston but lost all three decisions in July.

Mexico (6): Mel Almada

As early as 1908, with RHP Frank Arellanes, the Red Sox have had Mexican American ballplayers on the team, but the first player born in the Estados Unidos de Mexico joined the team in 1933, Tom Yawkey's first year as owner

Curt Fullerton (*left*) and Mel Almada, 1933. *Leslie Jones photograph, Boston Public Library*.

of the club. Baldomero Melo Almada came from the state of Sonora and the wonderfully named community of Huatabampo. He was, in fact, the first Mexican to play for any major-league team. Here, at least, the Red Sox were pioneers. His father had been appointed consul and served in Los Angeles. Almada was primarily an outfielder and played in parts of five seasons for the Red Sox, 1933 into mid-June 1938. His most active year was 1935, when he appeared in 151 games and hit .290 with 59 RBIs and 85 runs scored. Other Mexican natives on the Red Sox are Vicente Romo (1969), Carlos Rodriguez (1994), Alfredo Aceves and Dennys Reyes (both in 2011), and Hector Velasquez (2018–19).

Netherlands: Win Remmerswaal

The one and only native of the Netherlands was the Hague's Remmerswaal, a right-handed pitcher who did win—once—in his first year with Boston, in 1979. In 1980, he again was called up midseason and booked a couple more wins against just one loss. In 22 appearances, he was 3-1 (5.50 ERA).

Nicaragua (3): Devern Hansack.

The pride of Pearl Lagoon, Davern Hansack remains a personal favorite for a game the author saw on the last day of the 2006 season. A RHP, Hansack had lost his debut about a week before. This day at Fenway, he threw a no-hitter against the Orioles. His game is not to be found among the lists of no-hitters, however, because it lasted only five innings before the game had to be called due to rain. The game is listed as a shutout, which it was, and a complete game. He got a win. He didn't give up any hits. He walked one batter in the second and struck out six. Hansack was 0-1 in 2007

Fenway Park tarp ready for a rain delay. It was rolled out when Devern Hansack threw his no-hitter on the last day of 2006. *Bill Nowlin photo.*

(but was given a world championship ring) and 1-0 in 2008. The other two Nicaraguans were Vicente Padilla (2012) and Erasmo Ramirez (2019).

Panama (3): Ben Oglivie
In 2003, there were two Panamanians on the Red Sox: Ramiro Mendoza and Bruce Chen, though Chen was with the team for less than three weeks in May. Mendoza was with the Sox both in 2003 and 2004. The first, though, was Ben Oglivie, from Colon, in 1971. He broke into the big leagues with Boston and played left field in 166 games from 1971 to 1973 (appearing in 94 games in 1972). He hit .235 for the Red Sox but enjoyed much better success in thirteen seasons after leaving Boston, playing for Detroit and Milwaukee.

Poland: Johnny Reder
The palindromic Reder was a national soccer star before playing baseball for the Boston Red Sox. He's one of only four Poles to play in the majors. In April, May, and the first half of June, Reder appeared in 17 games for the 1932 Red Sox (the team that finished the season 45-109), but Reder hit just .135 in 43 plate appearances, with 3 RBIs. (Readers might anticipate that a gratuitous note about the Pesky Pole would be inserted here, but Johnny's parents came from Croatia.)

Puerto Rico (30): José Santiago

Puerto Rico is, of course, not a country but part of the United States. It does have a distinct culture of its own, however, and a great deal of territorial pride. When manager Alex Cora led the 2018 Red Sox to a World Series win, in his first year as manager, it was an occasion to celebrate across the island. Cora had played for the Red Sox in 2005–7, winning his first ring in '07. Of the twenty-nine Puerto Ricans who have played for the Red Sox, the first was José Santiago back in 1966. He came to Boston from the Kansas City A's and won 12 games both in 1966 and in the "Impossible Dream" year of 1967. His 12-4 record in 1967 earned him the league's lead in winning percentage. It also earned him the start in Game One of that year's World Series against the St. Louis Cardinals. He might well have won that game but for a lack of run support. In his two starts, his teammates scored a total of zero runs. Game One was a 2–1 loss to Bob Gibson, the only Red Sox run coming on Santiago's own solo home run. He got hit hard for four runs and didn't last out the inning in Game Four, as the Sox were shut out, 6–0.

Saudi Arabia: Alex Wilson

Right-handed pitcher Alex Wilson's father, Jim, had worked as a geologist for Aramco, and Alex was born in Dhahran just a few days after the Red Sox lost Game Seven of the 1986 World Series. Alex himself was a second-round pick of the Sox in 2009 and appeared in 26 games with the World Champion 2013 team; he was 1-1 and did not appear in the postseason. He spent most of 2014 in the minors but was 1-0 (1.91) in eighteen appearances. After the season, he was involved in the trade that brought New Jersey native Rick Porcello to Boston.

Scotland: Bobby Thomson

Glaswegian Bobby Thomson was famous forever for his "shot heard 'round the world" home run that won the 1951 pennant for the New York Giants. In December 1959, the Red Sox traded Al Schroll to acquire him. In 40 games in 1960, he hit .263 with 20 RBIs and was given his release on July 1. After signing on with the Orioles, he appeared in 3 hitless games and retired from baseball later in the month.

Taiwan (2): Che-Hsuan Lin

Both Taiwanese players the Red Sox have fielded share the same surname, the not-uncommon Lin. Che-Hsuan Lin was the first, in 2012. In contests at the beginning and end of the season, he played 3 games in center and

6 games in right. He had a total of 12 at-bats and had 3 base hits, without a run batted in. After the season, he was placed on waivers. His story still in progress, Tzu-Wei Lin appeared in 25 games for the 2017 Red Sox and 37 games for the World Champion 2018 team. He appeared in 13 early-season games for the 2019 Sox.

Venezuela (35): Luis Aparicio

Perhaps surprisingly, Venezuela has provided more ballplayers to the Boston Red Sox than any other country except the Dominican Republic. The first player from the Bolivarian Republic of Venezuela to play for the Red Sox was future Hall of Famer Luis Aparicio (1971–73), the last three seasons of his career. The Rookie of the Year in 1956 (with the White Sox), the superb shortstop had already been named to ten All-Star squads and had earned eight Gold Gloves before he came to Boston. He was an All-Star two more times, in 1972 and 1973. Pitcher Eduardo Rodriguez (19-6 in 2019) is the most recent true star from Venezuela.

Virgin Islands (3): Joe Christopher

Like Puerto Rico, the U.S. Virgin Islands (as distinct from the British Virgin Islands) is a territory of the United States. Its citizens are U.S. citizens. Three of them have played for the Boston Red Sox. The first (and most noted) was Joe Christopher, though his bigger claim to fame was for being a member of the original 1962 New York Mets. He'd broken in as a part-time player for the Pirates but from 1962 through 1965 had played outfield for the Mets. He had 626 major-league games under his belt before he came to Boston for his final dozen. In those 12 games in 1966, Christopher hit just .077. Outfielder Midre Cummings (1998 and 2000) and first baseman Calvin Pickering (2001) are the other two Virgin Islanders who have played for the Red Sox.

Wales: Ted Lewis

The man from Machynlleth, Ted Lewis is briefly profiled at the beginning of this section.

FIRST FOREIGN-BORN MANAGER

The team's first foreign-born manager was a Canadian, Fred Lake, who hailed from Nova Scotia. He managed the final thirty-nine games of the

1908 season, succeeding Deacon McGuire, and all of 1909. In 1910, he managed Boston's other major-league team of the day, the National League's Braves (known that season as the Boston Doves).

Immediately succeeding Lake was another foreign-born manager, Patsy Donovan. He was born in Queenstown, County Cork, Ireland. He played seventeen years with a career .301 batting average. He already had nine years as a manager under his belt (the first eight of them as a player-manager) when he joined the Red Sox. He lasted two years with the Red Sox (1910 and 1911), seeing those teams do a little better than .500 each year. With Lake managing the Braves in 1910, both big-league teams in Boston had foreign-born managers.

Again noting that Puerto Rico is part of the United States, it is still worth observing that Alex Cora of Caguas managed the 2018 Red Sox to 108 regular-season wins in his first year as skipper. That team breezed through the postseason. Cora thus earned his second World Series ring with the Red Sox; he played 83 games with the 2007 World Champions, mostly at second base and shortstop. He has a third ring, thanks to coaching the Houston Astros in 2017. As events transpired, however, an investigation by Major League Baseball concluded early in 2020 found that Cora had been involved in sign-stealing operations during both 2017 and 2018, and a press statement said that he and the Red Sox had "mutually agreed to part company."

A FOREIGN-BORN TEAM OWNER

The Red Sox have also had one foreign-born owner: Joseph J. Lannin was born in 1866 in Lac Beauport, Quebec, Canada. He owned the team for three years (1914–16) and saw them win the World Series in his second and third years. Had Tom Yawkey, his widow and the Yawkey Trust won two-thirds of the World Series during their combined sixty-nine years of ownership, the Red Sox would have forty-six more championships to the team's credit.

29

ONE-HIT WONDERS

Players with Only One Hit

There are forty-one players who had just 1 hit in their big-league career and whose 1 hit was with the Boston Red Sox. Let's recognize them here.

Most are, unsurprisingly, pitchers, who don't often get as many opportunities to bat in the American League (the designated hitter was implemented in 1973). A relief pitcher might work a lengthy career and never once get a chance to bat.

If one separates out the twenty-two pitchers here, there are eighteen position players—and Chris Mahoney, who was both. The day on which he got his hit was a day on which he pitched. His hit was a single.

NAME	POSITION	YEAR OF HIT	NUMBER OF PLATE APPEARANCES FOR THE SOX
Bob Adams	P	1925	3
Kim Andrew	2B	1975	2
Tex Aulds	C	1947	4
Stew Bowers	P	1935	6
Frank Bushey	P	1930	9
Walter Carlisle	LF	1908	11
Swede Carlstrom	SS	1911	7
Ed Carroll	P	1929	20

NAME	POSITION	YEAR OF HIT	NUMBER OF PLATE APPEARANCES FOR THE SOX
Pete Charton	P	1964	11
Bob DiPietro	RF	1951	13
Vaughn Eshelman	P	1997	4
Joe Giannini	SS	1911	2
Andy Gilbert	CF	1942	15
Dave Gray	P	1964	1
Guido Grilli	P	1966	2
Bobby Guindon	PR, 1B, LF	1964	9
Hy Gunning	1B	1911	10
Alex Hassan	RF, PH, DH	2014	9
Tom Herrin	P	1954	8
Harley Hisner	P	1951	2
Les Howe	P	1924	8
Ben Hunt	P	1910	19
Brian Johnson	P	2018	6
Joe Kiefer	P	1926	7
Hal Kolstad	P	1963	22
Walt Lynch	C	1922	2
Alejandro Machado	OF, PR, 2B	2005	6
Chris Mahoney	P, RF	1910	9
Spike Merena	P	1934	10
Doc Moskiman	PH, 1B, RF	1910	11
Ken Poulsen	PH, 3B, SS	1967	5
Ralph Pond	CF	1910	4
Frank Quinn	P	1949	6

RED SOX IN 5S AND 10S

Name	Position	Year of Hit	Number of plate appearances for the Sox
Al Richter	SS, PH	1951	14
Len Swormstedt	P	1906	8
Blaine Thomas	P	1911	2
Tony Tonneman	C	1911	7
Ben Van Dyke	P	1912	4
Dana Williams	PR, LF	1989	6
John Wilson	P	1910	10
Clarence Winters	P	1924	3

30

ONE-WIN WONDERS

Pitchers with Only One Win

Not wanting to unduly embarrass pitchers who gave it a try, we will list just three pitchers here. It seems like a surprisingly small number; there are sixteen pitchers who threw for the Red Sox and won one time—but only one time—for the team. Some, like Lefty O'Doul in 1923, won once and lost once. Seven of them were 1-0 (Chris Carpenter, Guy Cooper, Robert Manuel, Vince Molyneaux, Chris Smith, Carlos Valdez, and Jermaine Van Buren). Chris Smith was 1-4 for his career but an unblemished 1-0 for the 2008 Red Sox.

We should celebrate the ones who were undefeated, but we admit to being a bit more fascinated by three pitchers who wrapped up their Red Sox career 1-6.

1. Steve Ellsworth (1-6, 1988)
Lefty Dick Ellsworth was 16-7 for the Red Sox in 1968, the only year of his thirteen big-league seasons he had a decision for Boston. His eight-year-old son Steve played in that year's Red Sox Fathers and Sons game. Twenty years later, Steve, a six-foot, eight-inch righty, pitched for the Red Sox. He'd signed with the team in 1981 and spent seven years in the minors. When he made the major-league team, he started the third game of the season but was bombed for five runs in the first two innings; he bore the loss. He won his third start, 12–3. But as his record indicates, he was 1-6 on the season with a 6.75 ERA, for a team that finished first in the AL East. He was up and down to Pawtucket a couple of times, but his last appearance in the majors was on July 2.

2. John Michaels (1-6, 1932)

Michaels was a left-hander who appeared in 28 games for the 1932 Red Sox, arguably the worst team in franchise history. The team finished with a 43-109 record. Michaels didn't have the worst record on the team—Gordon Rhodes was 1-8, and Jack Russell was 1-7. Michaels's ERA was somewhat average for the team: 5.13 (team average, 5.02). One game he lost in June was because his teammates committed five errors behind him. In a game six days later, he led 2–1 heading into the ninth, but again poor defense cost him the game. His one win came against the Yankees, 6–5, and he allowed neither Lou Gehrig nor Babe Ruth to get a hit. In fact, for the rest of his life, he could always boast of striking out the Babe.

3. Ed Barry (1-6 over three seasons; 1-2 in 1905, 0-3 in 1906 and 0-1 in 1907)

Yet another left-hander, Ed Barry joined the team in late August 1905. He pitched in 7 games with a 2.88 ERA but was 1-2, winning a game against Cleveland on October 3. The next year (the execrable 1906 season), he appeared in only 3 games—and lost every one of them. They brought him back in 1907, long enough to get into 2 games, and he lost the only decision he had.

THE EXCEPTIONALLY STRANGE CASE
OF JOE HARRIS

Ed Barry's story notwithstanding, let's consider the story of Joe Harris. Their careers overlapped. Harris was also 1-2 in 1905. But in 1906, he was an astonishing 2-21. And the team signed him to pitch again in 1907! In that third year, Harris was 0-7. And Boston brought him to spring training again in 1908. He didn't make the team. How can we understand signing him again for 1907?

First of all, the team as a whole stunk in 1906—they finished in last place with a record of 49-105, 45½ games out of first. One of the features of the season was a 20-game losing streak. In 8 of the games Harris lost, the team was shut out. To quote his biographer, "In another six of Harris's losses, Boston scored just one run. Thus in 14 of the 21 games he lost, Boston batters scored a grand total of six runs. It's a little hard to win under those circumstances."[25]

There was one game he pitched that we'll never see again: on September 1, 1906, he and Jack Coombs of the Athletics squared off, and both of them pitched for twenty-four innings. Boston lost, 4–1. But he'd pitched twenty-three innings of one-run baseball, and he struck out 15 batters in the game.

Even fellow teammate Cy Young lost 21 games in 1906, but Young won 13. Harris had 1 shutout to his credit that year; Cy Young had 0.

PLACES THE RED SOX HAVE PLAYED BASEBALL

On June 29 and 30, 2019, the Red Sox played the Yankees in London, the first major-league baseball games ever played in Europe.

Over the years, including exhibition games, the Red Sox have played baseball in forty-two of the fifty United States, the District of Columbia, Puerto Rico, the Virgin Islands, three Canadian provinces (Ontario, Quebec, and New Brunswick), Cuba, the Dominican Republic, Japan, and Mexico.

Hope still remains that the Red Sox could become the first major-league team to play in all fifty states, to suggest that the team in this regard is truly "America's team." The eight states still awaiting a Red Sox visit are Alaska, Hawaii, Idaho, Montana, North Dakota, Oregon, South Dakota, and Wyoming.

J.D. Martinez taking batting practice in London's Olympic Stadium, June 2019. *Bill Nowlin photo.*

IX

THE BEST OF THE BEST

33

TOP 10 SEASONS OF INDIVIDUAL PLAYERS (PITCHERS AND BATTERS)

Any ranking of the best seasons of all Red Sox players needs to include offense, pitching, and fielding. Let's look at WAR first. The pitchers we have seen in chapter 10 and need not go over the details of their seasons again here, but five position players have edged into the top 10. Three of them are named Ted Williams. We will deal just with the nonpitchers here.

1. Cy Young (1901, 12.6)
See chapter 10.

2. Carl Yastrzemski (1967, 12.5)
This shouldn't be surprising. Yaz's 1967 season was already seen as legendary at the time. In 2005, the Red Sox declared David Ortiz the "clutchest Red Sox hitter of all time." It would be hard to match what he did in the 2004 postseason. But they may have forgotten Carl Yastrzemski. The 1967 pennant race was decided only on the final day of the season, and even when the Red Sox won during the final day game, 5–3, at Fenway Park on October 1, eliminating the Twins, they had to wait for the second of two games in Detroit. If the Tigers won, they'd be tied with the Sox. They lost, and the Sox finished one game ahead of the Twins and the Tigers. The Red Sox had had to win both of their last two games in order to clinch. They did, and Yastrzemski was 7-for-8 in the two games, with 6 RBIs. He also played superb defense. In the stretch run, in the final ten games of 1967, Yaz had 20 base hits (9 of them for extra bases) with 14 runs batted in. In the 6-4 win

on September 30, four of the team's runs were ones he drove in, and in the October 1 game, two of the team's five runs were his. He led the league with a .326 batting average; his .416 on-base percentage led both leagues, as did his 121 RBIs. His 44 homers tied him with the Twins' Harmon Killebrew; they both led the league. Yaz won the Triple Crown in 1967. He got nineteen of the twenty first-place votes for MVP.[26]

3. Pedro Martínez (2000, 11.7)
See chapter 10.

4. Smoky Joe Wood (1912, 11.4)
See chapter 10, keeping in mind that Wood's ranking includes a fairly significant dose of offense.

5. Mookie Betts (2018, 10.9)

Mookie Betts was presented both the Silver Slugger and Gold Glove for his 2018 MVP season. Photo taken at Fenway, April 2019. *Bill Nowlin photo.*

Betts had a spectacular season, the second-highest Wins above Replacement score ever attained by a Red Sox position player. He captured his third Gold Glove, won his second Silver Slugger, was named the Most Valuable Player in the American League (with twenty-eight first-place votes) and helped lead the team to its fourth World Championship in a fifteen-year stretch. His .346 batting average led both leagues, as did his 129 runs scored and his .640 slugging percentage. He is the only player in baseball history to attain all five accomplishments in one season: World Series victory, the MVP, the batting title, a Silver Slugger and a Gold Glove. 'Nuf said.

6. Ted Williams (1946, 10.9)
I could write books and books about Ted Williams. In fact, I already have—six or seven of them, with another one or two in the works. A good case could be made that his greatest season was 1957, because it was the year he turned thirty-nine and hit .388. Just 5 more base hits and he would have had a second .400 season. He was walked intentionally 33 times. Mickey

Mantle edged him out for the MVP in 1957, but not by much: 233 points to 209. He did get a 9.7 WAR. But we're not here to look at 1957. We are here to look at 1946. And, later in this list, 1941 and 1942. In 1946, the Red Sox won the pennant for the one and only time during the 1939–60 stretch when the "Kid" played for the Sox. He had missed all of 1943, 1944, and 1945 for military service. Rusty his first year back? He hit .342, homered 38 times and drove in 123 runs. He scored even more runs than he drove in, leading both leagues with 142 runs scored. In part, that was because he got on base so often. He drew 156 walks, 29 of them intentionally— though pitching carefully to Ted Williams earned him any number of what might be called semi-intentional walks. He got on base more than anyone else in either league. His OBP of .497 couldn't be very much closer to .500. Basically, he reached base almost 50 percent of the time he came to bat. That was true throughout his career. His career .482 on-base percentage is tops of all time. He did win the MVP in 1946, the first of two MVP awards. He wuz robbed at least one other time; see his entry for 1942 later in this list. It's only unfortunate that an elbow injury hampered him in the one World Series he got to play in.

7. Lefty Grove (1936, 10.7)
See chapter 10.

8. Wes Ferrell (1935, 10.6)
See chapter 10. Like Smoky Joe Wood, Ferrell's overall player WAR is presented here, not just his WAR as a pitcher.

9. Ted Williams (1941, 10.6)
This was, of course, the year that twenty-two-year-old Ted Williams hit for a .406 batting average. No one has hit .400 since 1941. Had the sacrifice fly rule been in effect, he would have batted .411. His on-base percentage was .553. There was power as well as average; his 37 home runs led both leagues. Thanks to an equally impressive 56-game hitting streak, and the fact that the Yankees beat the Red Sox for the pennant (by seventeen games), New York's Joe DiMaggio was awarded the MVP.

10. Ted Williams (1942, 10.6)
Ted Williams led the majors once more, in many categories: batting average (.356), on-base percentage (.499), slugging (.648), homers (36), RBIs (137), runs scored (141), and total bases (338). It was the first year in which he won

the Triple Crown; he won it again in 1947. The Red Sox finished second to the Yankees once again, but by nine games, not seventeen. Once again, though, Williams came up second in MVP voting—to Joe Gordon of the Yankees. It was a travesty. Gordon must have been pretty amazing to have beaten someone who led in so many categories, right? What did Gordon lead in? Just two things. He struck out more than anyone in baseball. And he led the league in the number of times he grounded into double plays. That's it. Ted hit exactly twice as many homers, hit for 34 points higher in average and drove in 34 more runs. Gordon did make it to the World Series, though—but his batting average there was .095 with no runs batted in. That's not to say he hadn't been a good player in 1942; his WAR was 8.2. One does wonder how Williams would have done had he not lost the next three years due to World War II. He averaged 31.75 homers from 1939 to 1942 and 34.5 homers per year the next four after the war. Right there, he arguably lost 99 career home runs.

And Ted Williams was numbers 11, 12, and 13, too, right? No, his next-best season was 1947 with a 9.9 WAR. Number 11 on this list is Carl Yastrzemski (10.5, 1968). Number 12 is Roger Clemens (10.4, 1940). And number 13 is Babe Ruth (10.4, 1916).

Slumps

The best batting average for a Red Sox player was Ted Williams's .406 in 1941. The second-best was Ted's .388 in 1957. In 1912, Tris Speaker hit .383. Nomar Garciaparra is fourth, with his .372 in the year 2000. Fifth was Ted Williams, .369 in 1948. In 1932, the acquired-during-the-season Dale Alexander hit .367 overall, but for the Red Sox he hit .372.

The longest hitting streak for a Sox player belongs to Dom DiMaggio, 34 games in 1949. Nomar hit in 30 consecutive games in 1997, replicating the 30-game streak Tris Speaker recorded in 1912. In 2016, Jackie Bradley Jr. hit in 29 straight games. Johnny Damon hit for 29 games in 2005.

What about slumps, though? Maybe we ought to acknowledge them. They happen. One happened to Luis Aparicio in 1971. He was 0-for-44 until he snapped the streak on June 1. It had gotten so bad (for the future Hall of Famer) that even U.S. president Richard M. Nixon reached out to wish him well. George Scott had an 0-for-36 slump in 1978. If he'd stretched it a bit longer, maybe he'd have gotten a call from a president, too.

Red Sox Hall of Famer Dom DiMaggio taking a breather in the dugout at Fenway. *Leslie Jones photograph, Boston Public Library.*

In 1962, Chuck Schilling started the season 0-for-25. When he finally singled, on April 19 (the season was nine days old), he drove in a run, but—perhaps unaccustomed as he was with first base—he was picked off shortly afterward, ending the inning.

Lou Clinton had gone 0-for-21, but on August 12, 1963, he broke out. Facing future Hall of Famer Jim Kaat, he hit a three-run homer and then, his next time up, he hit a two-run homer off Kaat. Slump over.

CONSECUTIVE GAMES ON BASE SAFELY

Affectionately known as CGOBS, this record is owned by Ted Williams. Almost every baseball fan knows that back in 1941, the Yankees' Joe DiMaggio had a 56-game hitting streak. What almost no fans know is that Ted Williams owns another, similar streak that was much longer. Getting a base hit is, of course, a very good thing for a batter to do. A home run or a double is better than a single, but even a single gets the batter on base and maybe advances one or more runners who already occupy a bag. Ted Williams was an extremely disciplined batter. As we know, his mantra was "Get a good pitch to hit," and he refused to swing at bad pitches. He walked more than 20 percent of the time he came to the plate. A walk also puts a batter on base. A walk can advance a runner on first; it can even force in a run if the bases are loaded. Ted walked at a higher percentage than anyone who ever played the game, and his .482 career on-base percentage is the highest of anyone who ever played.

SABR researcher Herm Krabbenhoft knew that Joe DiMaggio had, after those 56 consecutive games in which he got a hit, walked in game number 57 and then started a new hitting streak that lasted 16 more games. Including the base on balls, he had reached base safely in 73 consecutive games. (As it happens, he had walked in the game before the hitting streak began, so Joe D had actually reached base in 74 consecutive games.)

Naturally, Herm was curious. Had anyone ever done better? Yes. In 1949, Ted Williams topped Joltin' Joe. On July 1, he singled and drove in a run. In every game he played in July (31 of them), Ted reached base safely. In every game he played in August (also 31 of them), Ted reached base safely. And in the first 22 games he played in September—all the way through September 27—he reached base safely. That totaled 84 games in which, one way or another, he had reached base.

So, Ted Williams had an 84-game CGOBS streak.

As I've written previously: "Throughout his entire career, if one excludes games in which he had only one plate appearance, as a pinch hitter, there were only seven times from 1939 through 1960 that he failed to get on base safely two games running. And only once (in 1939) did Williams fail to get on base three games in a row (May 23–25, 1939). On August 20, 1939, Williams didn't get on base in either game of a doubleheader. In 1940, he failed in the second game of a July 13 doubleheader and in the first game of the next day's doubleheader. Both days he reached safely in the other game.

Ted Williams arrives at a SABR symposium in Crystal River, Florida, to discuss "Shoeless" Joe Jackson. *Bill Nowlin photo.*

"From July 14, 1940 through September 26, 1950—more than a full decade—Williams never once had back-to-back games without reaching safely, if a pinch-hit appearance in 1941 and another in 1948 are discounted."[27]

This (1949) was a year in which he played in every game all season long, led the league in homers and RBIs (tied with teammate Vern Stephens with 159) and won the MVP. He would have won the

Triple Crown had the Tigers' George Kell not nosed him out for the batting title, .3429118 to Ted Williams's .3427561, a margin of .0001557, one-thousandth of a point.[28]

Joe DiMaggio's CGOBS streak was 74 games. Ted Williams is not only number 1 but also ranks number 3 and number 4, reaching base safely in 69 straight games in 1941 and in 65 straight games in 1948.

During his 1949 streak, there were 14 games in which Williams did not get a base hit. But in those games, he walked 23 times. And over those 84 games, he collected 111 base hits. Between walks and hits, he reached base 134 times. He was not hit by a pitch during the streak.

REACHING BASE SAFELY IN 16 CONSECUTIVE PLATE APPEARANCES

Ted Williams did this in 1957, not long after he turned thirty-nine years old on August 30.

> *September 17 vs. KC, pinch-hit home run*
> *September 18 vs. KC, pinch-hit walk*
> *September 20 at NY, pinch-hit home run*
> *September 21 at NY, home run, three walks*
> *September 22 at NY, home run, single, two walks*
> *September 23 at NY, single, three walks, hit by pitch*

Since a walk is not considered an at-bat, SABR's Cliff Otto points out that this string includes four home runs in four consecutive official at-bats.

34

ALL-TIME STARTING LINEUP

We've lingered—maybe too long—on some of the worst Red Sox teams of all time. Not a lot was expected of some of those teams. One could also consider which were the most disappointing Red Sox teams. How do we measure this? 1948, 1949, 1978? 2003? Or teams like the last-place teams of 2012 and 2014, during a stretch when so much more was expected of those teams? Maybe we just won't worry about that here. Let's focus on the positive. Let's come up with an imaginary team: the best hypothetical Red Sox team of all time.

POSITION PLAYERS

3B	Wade Boggs
CF	Tris Speaker
LF	Ted Williams
DH	David Ortiz
1B	Carl Yastrzemski
2B	Bobby Doerr
SS	Joe Cronin
RF	Harry Hooper
C	Jason Varitek

PITCHERS

Starting RHP	Pedro Martínez
Starting LHP	Jon Lester
Second RHP	Roger Clemens

Tim Wakefield won 186 games for the Red Sox and threw 26 complete games. *Bill Nowlin photo.*

Second LHP	Lefty Grove
Main Reliever	Bob Stanley
Secondary Reliever	Mike Timlin
Secondary Reliever	Dick Radatz
Closer	Jonathan Papelbon
	Cy Young
	Tim Wakefield
Postseason pitchers	Babe Ruth, Curt Schilling

ALL-TIME SECOND TEAM

Bench catcher	Carlton Fisk
Bench infielder	Jimmie Foxx
Bench infielder	Nomar Garciaparra
Bench outfielder	Jim Rice
Bench outfielder	Jackie Jensen
Bench DH	Manny Ramirez
Other outfielders	Fred Lynn, Dwight Evans and Tris Speaker

Tempted as we were to come up with an all-time worst team, we decided that would be too unkind, even if most of the players might have been from the dismal decade of the 1920s. And, yes, I know: choices like Varitek over Fisk were really difficult to make.

35

BEST GAMES AGAINST THE YANKEES

There can't be much doubt about the top 4 on this list. They came one after the other in October 2004. The way it all unfolded made it as special a run as one could dream up. The Red Sox had won the World Series in 1918 but then not won another one since. Meanwhile, the rival Yankees had won the World Series in 1923, 1927, 1928, 1932, 1936, 1937, 1938, 1939, 1941, 1943, 1947, 1949, 1950, 1951, 1952, 1953, 1956, 1958, 1961, 1962, 1977, 1978, 1996, 1998, 1999, and 2000. It's pretty impressive when typed out like that.

To make matters worse, the 1949 Yankees had eliminated the Red Sox in the final game of the year. Had the Red Sox won either of their last two games, they would have won the pennant. They won neither. In 1978, the Yankees and Red Sox squared off in a single-game playoff for the pennant, at Fenway Park. The Yankees won it. In 2003, the Red Sox and Yankees played a seven-game American League Championship Series. Whoever won Game Seven would go to the World Series. Heading into the bottom of the eighth, the Red Sox held a reasonably comfortable 5-2 lead. The Yankees won in eleven innings.

So, in 2004, when the two teams faced off once more in the ALCS and Boston lost the first two games, at Yankee Stadium, 10–7 and 3–1, their only hope was that coming home to Fenway Park for three games would give them fresh life. Instead, they got slaughtered, losing 19–8. There was no reason for any hope at this point.

Game Four was on Sunday night. After four innings, the Yankees led, 2–0. Was there really any reason for a Red Sox fan to go on living?

A certified Yankees hater at a game in Boston. *Bill Nowlin photo*.

Then, a moment of hope: the Sox scored three runs in the bottom of the fifth, Orlando Cabrera driving in one and David Ortiz driving in two. But minutes later, the Yankees re-took the lead, albeit by just one run, with two runs in the top of the sixth. The Sox went down 1-2-3 in the sixth and seventh. And then the Yankees brought in Mariano Rivera. He gave up a single but then retired the next three. The game went into the bottom of the ninth. TVs were turned off all across New England; people just didn't want to see it: swept by the Yankees.

No. Kevin Millar walked. Pinch-runner Dave Roberts stole second. (Roberts got a standing ovation at Fenway Park in 2018, when he was manager of the Los Angeles Dodgers facing the Red Sox in that year's World Series.) And Bill Mueller singled to center, tying the game. Extra innings followed. The Yankees loaded the bases in the top of the eleventh but couldn't score. In the bottom of the twelfth, at 1:22 a.m., David Ortiz hit a two-run homer. The Red Sox had survived.

The win occurring well after midnight, it was only fifteen hours and forty-nine minutes until Game Five got underway. Game Five lasted even longer than Game Four, five hours and forty-nine minutes, as opposed to five hours and two minutes. It also saw just a bit of a seesaw. The Yanks led, 4–2, after six, but the Sox tied it in the bottom of the eighth. This one went into extra innings, beyond the twelve innings of Game Four, all the way to the fifteenth. With a strikeout, a walk, and another strikeout, it looked like we were going to the sixteenth, but then Manny Ramirez drew another walk, pushing Johnny Damon into scoring position at second base with David Ortiz leaving the on-deck circle and stepping into the batter's box. He kept fouling off pitches, until finally, on the tenth pitch of the at-bat, Ortiz singled to center field and scored Damon. It was still before midnight, the game ending on the same calendar day as the extra-inning Ortiz game-winner of Game Four.

The two back-to-back losses seemed to break the Yankees. The ALCS moved back to Yankee Stadium. All they had to do was win either game, but in Game Six, the Red Sox scored four runs in the fourth inning, three of them on a home run by second baseman Mark Bellhorn (who had led the league in strikeouts). Curt Schilling, with blood from a surgical procedure just a couple of days before leaking through his socks and staining them red, allowed just one run in seven innings, and the bullpen did the rest.

And in Game Seven, it was pretty much all over early. Ortiz homered for 2 runs in the first inning, and Johnny Damon hit a grand slam in the second. When the Yankees had the temerity to score once in the third, Damon came back up and hit another home run in the top of the fourth, making it 8–1 Red Sox. The final score was 10–3. And the Red Sox then swept the St. Louis Cardinals in the World Series.

The Yankees did win one more World Series, in 2009. The Red Sox won three more in the current century: 2007, 2013, and 2018.

Five Other Great Red Sox/Yankees Games

It's really true that a contest like the 1978 playoff game was a "great game" in that, forty years later, those who are old enough to have lived through it still remember the details. But this being a partisan book, we elect to focus only on the games the Red Sox actually won.

1. October 10, 1904
The Boston Americans had won the American League pennant in 1903, in the third year of their existence, and then won the first-ever World Series,

beating the Pittsburg Pirates. In 1904, the Bostons hoped to repeat. A suddenly surging New York Highlanders team gave them a run for their money. Though Boston held first place for most of the season, they were in and out of first for most of September, and New York overtook them on October 7 with a 5–3 win. There were only four games left on the schedule, the two teams playing each other in back-to-back doubleheaders. Had they split the two games, New York would have captured the flag. Boston swept the first doubleheader, in Boston, by the disparate scores of a lopsided 13–2 and a 1–0 Cy Young shutout. The two teams decamped to New York to play two there on October 10. Now Boston had to win just one of the two. New York started 41-game-winner Jack Chesbro, but he'd been overworked, pitching on both October 7 and 8. New York scored twice off Bill Dinneen in the fifth, but Boston tied it up in the seventh. In the top of the ninth, a scratch infield hit, a sacrifice, an advance to third on another out, and then a wild pitch gave Boston a 3–2 lead, and they held it. They'd won the pennant again. The National League's New York Giants refused to play the upstart American League team in the postseason; it was only in 1905 that the World Series became an annual event.

2. August 17, 1947

The Red Sox had won the pennant with ease in 1946 but lost the World Series in seven. They were in second place in 1947 but a full thirteen and a half games behind the Yankees. Winning this game at Yankee Stadium accorded them some measure of pride. It was a battle of two starters, both of whom went the distance—Denny Galehouse for Boston and Vic Raschi for New York. And the distance was eleven innings. Through ten, the Red Sox had four hits and the Yankees five, but neither had scored a run. Birdie Tebbetts doubled to lead off the eleventh. Sam Dente, Sam Mele, and Johnny Pesky all singled, and the Sox scored three runs. Galehouse held the Yankees to win the game.

3. April 14, 1967

The twenty-one-year-old lefty, Billy Rohr, was given the honor of starting the third game of the Red Sox season, in Yankee Stadium. In 1966, neither team had done well. The Red Sox finished just a half game out of last place, spared the cellar only because the Yankees resided there. Who knew that the '67 Red Sox would win the pennant, in the Impossible Dream year? Rohr set down the first ten Yankees he faced but walked two in the bottom of the fourth. He walked another in the fifth and yet another in the sixth.

But through eight innings, he hadn't given up even one base hit, and Boston had scored three runs off Whitey Ford—a one-run leadoff homer by Reggie Smith and a two-run homer by Joe Foy. Catcher Russ Gibson had known it was a no-hitter in the making since the fourth. Rohr had almost given up a hit in the sixth; a hard-hit ball ricocheted off his shin but went right to third baseman Joe Foy, who threw the batter out. After five minutes of hobbling around, Rohr continued. He himself committed a throwing error in the eighth, but nothing came of it, and there were still no Yankee hits. Come the bottom of the ninth, Tom Tresh led off and hit a ball far over Yastrzemski's head in left field, but somehow Yaz caught it—a catch that broadcaster Ken Coleman called the greatest catch he had ever seen. Joe Pepitone flew out for the second out. Then Elston Howard singled over second base. Rohr got the next batter to fly out, too. He had pitched a one-hit shutout against the Yankees in Yankee Stadium in his major-league debut. Many in the crowd had begun rooting for Rohr, and Howard later said it was the first time a crowd had booed after he got a base hit in his home park.

4. September 10, 1999

Pedro Martínez (20-4) faced off against Andy Pettitte (12-10) at Yankee Stadium. The two teams were jockeying for first place in the AL East, but Boston was 6½ games behind New York. Pedro hit the first batter he faced, Chuck Knoblauch. He gave up a solo home run to Chili Davis in the bottom of the second. He struck out one in the first, two in the second, two in the third, but none in the fourth. In the fifth and in the seventh, he struck out the side. There'd been a strikeout in the sixth. Former Yankee Mike Stanley's two-run homer in the top of the sixth had given the Red Sox a one-run lead. In the bottom of the eighth, the first Yankee popped up foul. Then Pedro struck out each of the final five batters he faced (seven of the last eight), ending up with 17 Ks and a 2–1 win. No game in history had ever seen that many Yankees strike out. As Steve Buckley wrote in the *Boston Herald*: "Think about that. None of the great ones—Bob Feller, Walter Johnson, Lefty Grove, Nolan Ryan—ever struck out 17 Yankees in a game."

5. October 16, 1999

The Red Sox finished second in 1999, then beat the Indians in the American League Division Series. That brought them to face the Yankees in the ALCS. They lost the first two games, 4–3 in ten innings in Game One and 3–2 in Game Two. For Game Three, the series came to Fenway Park. It looked like something of a match for the ages: Pedro Martínez (23-4, 2.07 ERA in the regular season, leading all of baseball in both categories) against Roger Clemens, who had won three Cy Young Awards for the Red Sox but then gone to the Blue Jays and won two more. Now, as of 1999, he was pitching for the Yankees, not exactly endearing himself to the crowd in Boston. It wasn't even close. The first batter Clemens faced tripled. The second homered. Clemens gave up two more in the second and pitched to just one batter in the third (Mike Stanley, as it happens) and was pulled from the game. Stanley scored, so Clemens was charged with five runs in two innings. Martínez, on the other hand, pitched seven innings, giving up just two hits and no runs, striking out twelve. The final score was 13–1, Red Sox. It was, though, the last game the Red Sox won, while the Yankees went on to win the World Series. But it was one shining light, still remembered.

PLAYERS WHO WERE CHAMPIONS WITH BOTH THE RED SOX AND THE YANKEES

Given that the Yankees have won twenty-seven World Championships and the Red Sox have won nine, one might assume there were a lot of players—Babe Ruth, for example—who have won titles with both teams. But there aren't that many. There have been fourteen players who, though not always on the World Series roster for the teams in question, at least played in the regular season for the championship teams.

PLAYER	TEAM AND YEAR	TEAM AND YEAR
Alfredo Aceves	Yankees 2009	Red Sox 2013
Joe Bush	Red Sox 1918	Yankees 1923
Kevin Cash	Red Sox 2007	Yankees 2009
Johnny Damon	Red Sox 2004	Yankees 2009
Eric Hinske	Red Sox 2007	Yankees 2009
Sam Jones	Red Sox 1916	Yankees 1923
Mike Lowell	Yankees 1998	Red Sox 2007
Carl Mays	Red Sox 1915, 1916, and 1918	Yankees 1923
Mike McNally	Red Sox 1915 and 1916	Yankees 1923

PLAYER	TEAM AND YEAR	TEAM AND YEAR
Ramiro Mendoza	Yankees 1998 and 1999	Red Sox 2004
Herb Pennock	Red Sox 1915 and 1916	Yankees 1923, 1927, 1928, and 1932
Babe Ruth	Red Sox 1915, 1916, and 1918	Yankees 1923, 1927, 1928, and 1932
Wally Schang	Red Sox 1918	Yankees 1923
Everett Scott	Red Sox 1915, 1916, and 1918	Yankees 1923

Mike Lowell, MVP of the 2007 World Series. *Bill Nowlin photo.*

The list would have only a few players on it had the Red Sox not provided so many of these players to the Yankees. Neither Johnny Damon, Eric Hinske, nor Ramiro Mendoza was dealt from one team to the other. All three entered free agency and signed where they wished. Alfredo Aceves, Kevin Cash, and Mike Lowell each similarly made their way through free agency; Aceves actually pitched for the Yankees (2008–10), then the Red Sox (2011–13), and then the Yankees again (2014).

Famously, the Red Sox sold Babe Ruth to the Yankees after the 1919 season for $100,000 on December 26, 1919.

Five months earlier, on July 30, 1919, the Sox sent Carl Mays to the Yankees to complete an earlier deal made on July 29. He was the player to be named later (named just one day later). The Red Sox had agreed to send a player to be named later for Bob McGraw, Allen Russell, and $40,000.

Almost exactly one year after the Ruth deal, on December 15, 1920, the Red Sox sent two other champions to New York. Mike McNally and Wally Schang were traded (with Harry Harper and Waite Hoyt) to the New York Yankees for Del Pratt, Muddy Ruel, Hank Thormahlen, and Sammy Vick.

A year after that, the transfer of championship talent resumed. On December 20, 1921, the Red Sox traded three of these eight players to the

Yankees, all in the same deal. They traded "Bullet" Joe Bush, "Sad" Sam Jones and Everett Scott to the Yankees for Rip Collins, Roger Peckinpaugh, Bill Piercy, Jack Quinn, and $100,000.

There was one other deal that involved the Red Sox sending championship players to the Yankees. It wasn't December 1922. It was January 30, 1923. They traded Herb Pennock to the Yankees for Norm McMillan, George Murray, Camp Skinner, and $50,000. For four years in a row—once a year like clockwork—Red Sox players who had won championships with Boston were dealt to New York. Of the twenty-five players who were on the first Yankees team that won the World Series (1923), six of them had been provided by the Red Sox.

There is no instance of the Yankees dealing a championship player to the Red Sox who then later won a World Series with Boston.

It's just a throwaway line, but it's interesting to note that the Yankees in the twenty-first century are 1-14 in terms of reaching the playoffs and winning the World Series. In each of the following years, the Yankees made it to the playoffs but were eliminated: 2001, 2002, 2003, 2004, 2005, 2006, 2007, 2010, 2011, 2012, 2015, 2017, 2018, and 2019. They won the World Series once: 2009.

The Red Sox are 4-6.

BEST RED SOX TEAM OF ALL TIME

This is a question posed to me while working on the book *Red Sox vs. Yankees* (with coauthor and lifelong Yankees fan David Fischer). The publisher put the two of us together to write a book about the rivalry between the two teams. One of the things he suggested was that we each select what we thought was the best team of all time. I had thought he might pick the legendary 1927 Yankees, with Babe Ruth and Lou Gehrig, but Dave surprised me and selected the 1998 Yankees. And he convinced me of his choice. Selecting the best Red Sox team of all time, in the immediate wake of the 108-win 2018 season, and the way that team worked through the three rounds of the postseason, losing only one game in each round, certainly raised them to the forefront of my thinking. But was proximity in time clouding my judgment? In the afterglow of the World Series win, was I being fully rational?

What were the other choices? As I wrote in that book, "Until the last month or so of the 2018 season, I would have selected the 2004 Red Sox. Many Sox fans still would. Partly to tweak Yankees fans but, really, because that's the way most Sox fans have felt since then. You finally overcome 86 years of seeming futility. Call it a 'curse' or whatever, the Red Sox could never win it all."[29] And in 2004, they did. After waiting eighty-six years since their last world championship.

Aside from 2004 and 2018, what other teams would I consider? Six obvious choices are as follows, in chronological order:

"108 wins": Fenway Park 2018 season. *Bill Nowlin photo.*

1. The 1912 Red Sox (105-47)

This was the team with the best regular-season wins percentage (.691) in Red Sox history; second-best was the 1946 Red Sox at .675, followed by the 1915 team at .669 and then the 2018 Red Sox at .667. The pennant race wasn't even close in 1912; the Red Sox (playing their first season in brand-new Fenway Park) finished 14 games ahead of the second-place Senators. When it came to the World Series, though, they faced really stiff competition from the 103-win New York Giants. Series competition was so tough that the best-of-seven series took eight games to resolve. (Game Two was an eleven-inning 6–6 tie.) Four of the games were decided by one-run margins, and the decisive Game Eight went into extra innings. That final game saw the Giants take a 2–1 lead in the top of the tenth, but then Christy Mathewson was victimized by a Fred Snodgrass error in center field, a walk, a game-tying single by Tris Speaker, an intentional walk, and then a sacrifice fly off the bat of Larry Gardner. This was the year Smoky Joe Wood was 34-5; he was pitching in relief in Game Eight and got the win, becoming 3-1 in World Series action. By the way, that other team in New York (the American League team soon known as the Yankees) finished in last place, 55 games behind the Red Sox.

2. The 1915 Red Sox (101-50)

This often-overlooked team ranks right up there. There was no superstar pitcher like Joe Wood—though Wood himself was 15-5 in '15. In fact, the team didn't even have a 20-game winner. The 1912 team had three of them

(Hugh Bedient and Buck O'Brien each won 20 on the nose), but in 1915, they had no pitcher lose more than eight. The 1915 squad featured Rube Foster (19-8), Ernie Shore (18-8), Babe Ruth (18-8), Dutch Leonard (15-7), and Joe Wood (15-5). They spread the wins around. They had a team ERA of 2.39. The "golden outfield" of Duffy Lewis in left, Tris Speaker in center, and Harry Hooper in right were all veterans of the 1912 club. Lewis led the team with 76 RBIs. Speaker was second with 69. A pitcher led the team in homers (Babe Ruth, with 4). Ruth didn't even pitch in the World Series against the Philadelphia Phillies, and in his only at-bat, he pinch-hit and grounded out unassisted to first base. When it came to that Series, one might think that the Red Sox had gotten crushed. They scored just seven runs over the course of the first four games. But they won three of them and then won the final Game Five, 5–4, thanks to a solo home run by Hooper in the top of the ninth.

3. The 1946 Red Sox (104-50)

With the Second World War behind them, a whole raft of veterans returned from military service. That was true of every team, of course, but the Red Sox excelled on the field of play. They set the franchise record for good starts—if you call a 21-3 record through May 10 a good start. Most people would. The Yankees were playing well, too, though, and were just five and a half games behind on that date. The Red Sox never left first place; all season long, there was just one day (April 24) when they weren't in first. They placed eight Red Sox players on that year's All-Star team. When they finished, they were a comfortable twelve games ahead of the second-place Detroit Tigers. Maybe too comfortable. There was a six-game losing streak in the first half of September, and they lost their final two games, too. They may have lost their competitive edge. There are teams like the 2007 Colorado Rockies that just, finally, run out of steam. The 1946 Red Sox whiled away most of September; manager Joe Cronin even told some of them they were free to take off five days, to actually leave the team in mid-September for a break rather than go on the road to Chicago and St. Louis.[30] Then they had to sit around idle while the St. Louis Cardinals and Brooklyn Dodgers played a couple of additional games to determine the National League pennant (the two teams had finished in a tie). The Sox scheduled a "tune-up" game with a number of American League players from other teams brought in to try to keep them in playing shape (among them Joe DiMaggio and Hank Greenberg). Ted Williams was the AL MVP that year with 38 homers and 123 RBIs. He was hit in the elbow by a Mickey Haefner pitch during the tune-up, and the elbow swelled up to almost double its usual size. It hampered him throughout the Series. Williams drove in a grand total of one run. The Sox lost in seven.

4. The 1967 Red Sox (92-70)

Wins aren't everything (though they almost are!). This year saw the Sox climb from having one foot in the cellar. They finished in ninth place in the ten-team league in 1966, 26 games behind the first-place Orioles. Only the Yankees were worse—a half game worse and in tenth place. But the '67 season saw them win twenty more games than the year before, and they had to win both of the final two games of the season to even have a shot at tying for the pennant. That they did and won it outright as the Tigers and Twins both lost their final games. This was the year Yaz won the Triple Crown and almost "willed" the Red Sox to a pennant. He was 23-for-44 at the end of the year and 7-for-8 with 6 RBIs in the final two "must-win" games. Coming out of something like nowhere, this was the "Impossible Dream" season, and it energized dormant baseball passion in New England. Attendance at home games more than doubled, from 811,172 in 1966 to 1,727,832 in 1967. The 1967 team has been credited ever since for giving birth to the phenomenon known as Red Sox Nation.

5. The 1975 Red Sox (95-65)

The 1975 team was a strong one. There was some jockeying for first place over the first couple of months, but from June 29 on the Red Sox secured and retained first place. There had been the disappointment in 1972, when the Sox finished just a half game out of first place (due to an unbalanced schedule because of a work stoppage at the start of that season). But in 1975, they beat second-place Baltimore by a reasonably comfortable four and a half games. They won at home, and they won on the road. They were 23-13 in one-run games. The Indians were the only team against which they had a losing record (7-11). They won twenty-four games by five or more runs. Having won the AL East, they swept the ninety-eight-win Oakland A's in the AL Championship Series. Fred Lynn and Jim Rice each drove in more than 100 runs; Lynn was named Rookie of the Year and Most Valuable Players in the American League. Up against the "Big Red Machine" Cincinnati Reds, they took the World Series to Game Seven after Carlton Fisk hit his majestic Game Six home run in the bottom of the twelfth in Game Six. Had Jim Rice not missed the entire postseason because of a fractured left hand suffered on September 21, he might well have provided the extra punch the Sox needed to win it all. They lost both Game Two and Game Seven by just one run.

6. The 1986 Red Sox (95-56)

Following an 81-81 season seeing the 1985 Red Sox finish fifth in the seven-team American League East, the 1986 team poured it on. It wasn't the easiest of seasons, but they did their thing again, and from May 14 to the end of the season they never lost their grip on first place. This was the year Roger Clemens was 24-4, among the 24 victories his first 20-K game. "Oil Can" Boyd won 16 games. Jim Rice drove in 110 runs. Bill Buckner drove in 102. Dwight Evans drove in 97. At the end, the Red Sox sat atop the AL East, with the Yankees 5½ games behind. The California Angels had won the AL West by five games. It was a hard-fought ALCS, with the Sox winning Game Two but the Angels holding a three-games-to-one edge after the first four games. And the Angels had a 5–2 lead heading into the ninth inning of Game Five. Don Baylor hit a two-run homer, and then Dave Henderson (Hendu!) hit a two-run homer to give the Sox a 6–5 lead. The Angels tied it in the bottom of the ninth. In the top of the eleventh, Baylor got hit by a pitch. Two singles followed, loading the bases. Hendu hit a sac fly scoring Baylor, and even though that was the only run they scored, the Sox held on. They won the next two games by big margins, 10–4 and 8–1. It was the Red Sox against the New York Mets in the World Series. Oddly, the home team lost every one of the first four games: two Mets losses in New York and then two Red Sox losses in Boston. The Sox won Game Five, 4–2. When they scored twice in the top of the tenth in Game Six and Calvin Schiraldi got the first two Mets in the bottom of the tenth to fly out, it looked like the long, long sixty-eight-year drought between World Series wins was over. And then it wasn't. We won't go into the details here. In Game Seven, just as in Game Seven of the 1975 World Series, they had a 3–0 lead against the Mets. And they blew it. Is it any wonder that there was fertile ground for the notion of a "Curse of the Bambino" that was going to deprive loyal Red Sox fans of another world championship, one way or another? The minute Dan Shaughnessy's *Curse of the Bambino* book came out, all Sox fans knew what the title would be. Wallowing in collective misery was something with which we had all had an abundance of experience.

THE FINAL FOUR ARE teams that couldn't have come much closer to winning it all. But for every single one of the four, they lost Game Seven of the World Series. It really is not surprising that when the notion of a "Curse of the Bambino" was floated, every Red Sox fan knew exactly what was meant.[31]

And it wasn't just those years. In 1948 and 1978, the Red Sox came as close to winning the pennant as possible, if one didn't actually win it outright:

they earned a single-game playoff for the pennant itself. Both playoff games were on the home field, at Fenway Park. Both times they lost, first to the Indians and second to the Yankees. Clearly, those were excellent teams, but it just didn't happen.

In 1949, the race to the pennant went down to the final two days. Had the Red Sox won either of the two final regular-season games (both at Yankee Stadium), they would have won the pennant. Did they? No, they lost them both—and the pennant—to the Yankees.

In 1972, the team finished a half game out of first place. How is that even possible? The Tigers (who finished first) played a different number of games than the Red Sox, because a strike at the beginning of the season (and the decision to play out the schedule from the day the strike ended, regardless of the number of games) had meant that the Tigers played one more game than the Red Sox. Detroit was 86-70, and Boston was 85-70. Again, just one more game at the end of the season made all the difference.

In 2003, it really seemed as though the Red Sox had the pennant in their pocket, leading the Yankees as they were in Game Seven of the American League Championship Series. The Sox were leading, 5–2, heading into the bottom of the eighth. All they needed was the final six outs, and they had a pair of superb and rested relievers in the bullpen. It didn't happen. Grady Little sent a tired, mentally checked-out Pedro Martínez back out there. (You can see video of Pedro in the dugout accepting congratulations from his teammates after finishing off the Yankees in the seventh.) The Sox lost in eleven innings.

Yes, there was every reason to think there had been a curse until 2004.

The 2004 Red Sox

We've already selected Games Four and Five of the ALCS as the two greatest Red Sox games ever played. We've seen (readers who were old enough in 2004 will never forget it) how the team rallied from being down three games to none in a best-of-seven series, coming back to win four games in a row, every one of the four games being a sudden-death game for the Red Sox (and winning those two extra-inning walk-offs). Given past history, as recent as 2003 but extending back to the four consecutive World Series in which they had lost the final game, who would expect a triumph? It had been eighty-six years. Red Sox fans were conditioned to expect the 2004 team to fall apart, too, but it never did. The "curse" had been reversed.

The 2007 Red Sox

And one could make a case that the 2007 Sox were one of the best teams of all time. From April 18 (just the thirteenth game of the season) through the end of the year, they never once were out of first place. (The 1946 Sox were in first from the tenth game of the season on.) But the 2007 team became world champions. They swept the Angels in the ALDS, fought through a seven-game ALCS against the Indians and then swept the Colorado Rockies in the World Series. A pretty dominant team!

The 2013 Red Sox

This was a very special team, too. After all, they won the World Series! Any team that does that is pretty special. The 2013 Red Sox won ninety-seven games, just one less than the 2004 squad. And they had their own cast of very special characters. That guy David Ortiz cropped up again: all he did was hit .688 in the World Series. The 2013 championship was sandwiched between last-place finishes in 2012 and 2014, with a last-place finish in 2015 as well.

The 2018 Red Sox

That was the team I chose. The final several weeks of the season were great fun. They had a lead of at least seven games over every other team in the AL East from August 29 to the end of the year. On the first of September, they had a record of 94-43. It didn't seem they could fail

This sign at Fenway Park displays the Red Sox's latest World Series victory. *Bill Nowlin photo.*

to win at least one hundred games. But all-too-frequently-snakebitten Red Sox fans who maybe still didn't believe 2004, 2007 and 2013 had ever really happened remained mentally steeled for a reversion to form, twentieth-century style. This was, though, a new century, and the 2018 team approached one hundred wins, hit it and then kept winning—108 wins in all. They blazed through the postseason as well, losing only one game in each of the three rounds of the postseason.

Those weren't easy postseason series, either. The ALDS was against the Yankees, who themselves had won one hundred games. The Red Sox took three out of four.

The ALCS was against the reigning World Champion Houston Astros, who had won 103 regular-season games. The Red Sox took four out of five. The World Series was against the Los Angeles Dodgers; they had won 102 regular-season games, then beat the Braves and the Brewers to earn their way into the World Series. So, the Sox beat three one-hundred-win teams.

Add them all up, they had 119 wins and 57 losses in 2018.

The 1912 team won 105 regular-season games. In 1915, the Sox won 101. The 1946 team won 104. But the 2018 Red Sox won 108. Adding in the postseason (there was only the World Series the three prior years, not the three rounds of postseason play that the 2018 Red Sox worked through), and the totals are as follows:

2018: 119 wins (.676 winning percentage, including 14 postseason games)

1912: 109 wins (.648 winning percentage, including 8 postseason games)

1946: 107 wins (.638 winning percentage, with 156-game regular season and 7 postseason games)

1915: 105 wins (.631 winning percentage, with 155 regular-season and 5 postseason games)

Large placards featuring Red Sox players' images to be carried on the duckboats during the 2018 World Series celebration. *Bill Nowlin photo.*

Looking back on the four World Series the Red Sox have won in the twenty-first century, they've kind of steamrollered their National League opponents, with sweeps in 2004 and 2007 and needing just six games in 2013 and five in 2018. That's a World Series total of 16 wins and 3 defeats. Over the course of the four World Series, the Red Sox have outscored their NL opponents by 56 runs. It's been a good stretch. I could have started this paragraph by writing: "Looking back on the four World Series the Red Sox have won (so far) in the twenty-first century…" But I didn't want to tempt fate. Red Sox fans who have lived through the many crushing defeats in the twentieth century and in 2003 don't feel any sense of entitlement—at least not the ones I know. They feel a sense of gratitude and appreciation. Until a better team comes along, though, I'll stick with the 2018 Red Sox as the greatest Sox team of all time.[32]

NOTES

Chapter 1

1. The full story is told in Chuck Burgess and Bill Nowlin, *Love That Dirty Water! The Standells and the Improbable Red Sox Victory Anthem* (Burlington, MA: Rounder Books, 2007), 126–28.

Chapter 3

2. In case you were wondering, Kevin Kouzmanoff had done the same thing with the Indians in September 2006. One pitch, four runs batted in.
3. The seven are Rube Kroh, Larry Pape, Buck O'Brien, Lefty Hockette, Dave Ferriss, Dave Morehead, and Billy Rohr.
4. Bill Nowlin, "Tony Conigliaro," SABR.org, https://sabr.org/bioproj/person/52ad9113.

Chapter 7

5. This author was present at the game.
6. There is a reason the author has a 2004 World Series baseball autographed by Dr. Morgan.

Chapter 10

7. MLB.com, mlb.com/glossary/standard-stats/walks-and-hits-per-inning-pitched.
8. Fangraphs, https://library.fangraphs.com/misc/war. Needless to say, a lot more information is available about WAR in various places, and different sites have their own ways of calculating WAR. For a very extensive look at how WAR is calculated, differences in calculations on various sites, and some discussion on the validity of the statistic—which everyone agrees is an approximation, despite looking very precise by virtue of its being presented with decimal places—visit https://www.baseball-reference.com/about/war_explained.shtml. For our purposes, we are using WAR as calculated by Baseball-Reference.com.

Chapter 11

9. For a complete listing of 20-game losers and a number of observations on the phenomenon, see Bill Nowlin and Emmet R. Nowlin, eds., *20 Game Losers* (Phoenix, AZ: SABR, 2017).

Chapter 12

10. Bill Nowlin, "Ben Flowers," SABR.org, https://sabr.org/bioproj/person/ae5a9e6c.
11. John F. Green, "Russ Kemmerer," SABR.org, https://sabr.org/bioproj/person/54e7c02b.

Chapter 13

12. Clif Keane, "Lynn's Day Began Sadly, Ended Sensationally," *Boston Globe*, July 19, 1975: 33.
13. Nate Taylor, "Nava Enjoys a Debut Loaded with Excitement," *Boston Globe*, June 13, 2010: C6. One can see the video on YouTube, https://www.youtube.com/watch?v=-9BLMdRRZ-s.
14. It had been done three times before in the majors—a grand slam in a first at-bat—but never two slams in a player's first two at-bats. The YouTube video is at https://www.youtube.com/watch?v=6af-1-amY6k.

Chapter 14

15. For anyone wishing to read about each of Ted Williams's 106 game-winning homers, they are detailed in Bill Nowlin, *521: The Story of Ted Williams' Home Runs* (Cambridge, MA: Rounder Books, 2013). Each home run—game-winner or not—is presented in this book.
16. Regan's first job in baseball was as a peanut vendor at Pittsburgh's Forbes Field. Readers who would like to learn more about Bill Regan are urged to read his biography. It's online and can be accessed at no charge. See Bill Nowlin, "Bill Regan," SABR BioProject, https://sabr.org/bioproj/person/445a5292.

Chapter 17

17. "Red Sox Win Out in Sensational Finish," *Boston Globe*, May 14, 1911, 1, 17.
18. Sam Otis, "Boston's 8 in 9th Keep Indians Out of First Place," *Plain Dealer*, June 9, 1937, 18.
19. Melville E. Webb Jr., "Red Sox Cut Loose for 8 Runs in Ninth, *Boston Globe*, June 8, 1937, 22.
20. Melville W. Webb Jr., "Cronin 4-Run Slam Puts Hex on Tigers," *Boston Globe*, August 6, 1938, 7.
21. Gerry Moore, "Williams' 10th Inning Hit Gives Sox Split—Braves Also Divide," *Boston Globe*, April 22, 1946, 6.
22. Burt Whitman, "Hose Rally in 9th of Second to Score 6 Runs," *Boston Herald*, July 31, 1931, 19, 20.

Chapter 19

23. Johnny Damon already had a single, double, and triple, but the out robbed him of the opportunity to hit for a cycle, all in one inning.

Chapter 23

24. The author was at Fenway Park on July 17, 1990, when the Red Sox hit into two 5-4-3 triple plays in the same game. The Red Sox won that game. It was the first time a team had ever hit into two triple plays in the same game.

Chapter 31

25. Bill Nowlin, "Joe Harris," SABR BioProject, https://sabr.org/bioproj/ person/2775e140.

Chapter 33

26. The other vote went to Minnesota's Cesar Tovar, who batted .267 and drove in 47 runs. He did score 98 runs.
27. Bill Nowlin, *Red Sox Threads* (Burlington, MA: Rounder Books, 2008), 462–64.
28. Herm and I once collaborated on another study, trying to see if even the slightest mistake might have occurred in the record-keeping of the day, thus earning Ted another batting title. Herm is a Tigers fan; I am a Red Sox fan. We couldn't find a sufficient error.

Chapter 36

29. Bill Nowlin and David Fischer, *Red Sox Vs. Yankees* (New York: Skyhorse, 2019), 225.
30. Among the players who took advantage of the "vacation" were the four "teammates" (Williams, Pesky, Doerr, Dom DiMaggio), a few pitchers, and even the manager—Cronin himself! See, among other sources, Mark Armour, *Joe Cronin* (Lincoln: University of Nebraska Press, 2010), 166.
31. Of course, it wasn't just a notion that was floated. It was embodied in a book: Dan Shaughnessy, *The Curse of the Bambino* (New York: Dutton, 1990).
32. As this book goes to press, a Major League Baseball investigation into alleged sign-stealing by the Red Sox had not yet concluded, but Alex Cora and the Red Sox had decided to "part company." Does the season thus require an asterisk? It's hard to say if we will ever know. The two last teams the Red Sox beat on their way to win the World Series, the Yankees and the Dodgers, had also been said to have engaged in sign-stealing as well.

ABOUT THE AUTHOR

Born in Boston, Bill Nowlin has not gone far in life. He lives on the other side of the river now, in Cambridge. Less than five miles from Fenway Park, he has been going to games there since the latter days of Ted Williams and right up to the present. One of the founders of Rounder Records and a former college professor of political science, he has spent much of the past twenty years writing about baseball. Since 2004, he has been on the board of directors of the Society for American Baseball Research. He's closing in on one hundred books at this point, mostly about baseball, many of them Red Sox–related.